The psychology of
judicial sentencing

Pour Thérèse Dupuis et Bob Pease

À tous deux, nous voulons exprimer notre amour et notre reconnaissance pour tout ce qu'ils nous ont donné

The psychology of judicial sentencing

Catherine Fitzmaurice and Ken Pease

Manchester University Press

Copyright © C. Fitzmaurice and K. Pease 1986

Published by Manchester University Press, Oxford Road, Manchester M13 9PL, UK
and
51 Washington Street, Dover, NH 03820, USA

British Library cataloguing in publication data
Fitzmaurice, Catherine
    The psychology of judicial sentencing.
    1. Sentences (Criminal procedure)—— England
    I. Title II. Pease, Ken
    344.205'772   KD8406

Library of Congress cataloging in publication data
Applied for

ISBN 0-7190-1819-6 *cased only*

Printed in Great Britain
at the Alden Press, Oxford

Contents

List of tables

List of figures

Acknowledgments

We are grateful to Phil Barnard for introducing us to the recent literature on cognitive psychology, to Leslie Wilkins, Andrew Ashworth, Andrew Mayes, Peter Ainsworth and Diana Bentley for reading chapters in draft and to Enid Roberts and Grace McCabe for helping with the tables throughout the book and for typing the early chapters.

Permission to reproduce material from other publications is gratefully acknowledged: to the National Institute of Justice, Washington DC for Table 1, to HMSO for Tables 3–5 and 12–14, to the *Journal of Criminal Law and Criminology* for Table 2, to the *International Journal of Criminology and Penology* for Table 6, to Heinemann for Table 10, Routledge and Kegan Paul for Table 11, and Martin Robertson for Tables 15 and 16.

Thanks are due to the *Prison Service Journal* for permission to reproduce some of the material in Chapter 7; to the Department of Social Work, Aberdeen University, for material in Chapter 9; to John Wiley for parts of Chapters 6 and 7, Table 9 and Figures 1, 3 and 4, and to the *Howard Journal* for Figure 2.

CHAPTER 1

Judges and psychologists

Man is a rational animal ... so at least I have been told. Throughout a long life, I have looked diligently for evidence of this statement, but so far I have not had the good fortune to come across it, though I have searched in many countries. (Russell, 1950)

A judge passing sentence thereby shows he has made a decision. It is an important decision, not only for the offender. A judicial sentence is an expression of power on behalf of society, made in its name. In most countries, including the United Kingdom, the more severe sentences are imposed by citizens acting alone. A distinguished judge, Lord Devlin (1979), wrote,

When I talk of the law-maker I mean a man whose business it is to make the law, whether it takes the form of a legislative enactment or of a judicial decision, as contrasted with the lawyer whose business it is to interpret and apply the law as it is. Of course the two functions often overlap; judges especially are thought of as performing both.

Atiyah (1983) stresses the amount of law which is made by lawyers rather than legislators.

In the United Kingdom, sentences are constrained by law in only one way, by specifying a maximum sentence. Maximum sentences are so severe as to be irrelevant to ordinary sentencing practice (Advisory Council on the Penal System, 1978). This is not surprising. The origins of the maxima lie in legislation restricting the scope of the death penalty during the second quarter of the nineteenth century (Thomas, 1978a, b). Judicial discretion has been further increased by the simplification of substantive law which David Thomas (1978a, b) identifies as the 'overriding legislative policy' of recent years. Judicial discretion increases as distinctions come to be made in the minds of sentencers rather than in statute. An appellate system is the obvious way of controlling judges' decisions. In the United Kingdom the appeal against judges' decisions is to other, more senior, judges.

In short, the judge has great freedom in his stewardship of power. Whether by default or intention, there is little challenge to his role. Yet, acting in concert, judges can subvert the penal purposes of the legislature. They can do this by discharging their powers to sentence in ways which the law permits. Recently, when attempts to reduce the use of custodial sentences have been made, increasingly frantically, by successive governments, the power of the judiciary to frustrate such attempts has been clear. This power makes an understanding of the psychology of judicial sentencing a matter of compelling practical interest. Little such understanding appears to exist. As the criminologist Don Gottfredson (1975) put it, 'it would be difficult to find other decision problems affecting critically the liberty and future and lives of large numbers of people in which decisions are made with so little knowledge of the way in which they are made'. Before justifying the involvement of psychologists in the analysis of sentencing decisions, let us first look at the lawyers' contribution to the literature on sentencing.

The legal literature on sentencing

Much of this literature has involved the articulation of general 'principles' of sentencing. For example, David Thomas's standard work (1979a) sets out the results of a detailed and penetrating examination of the decisions of the Court of Appeal (Criminal Division) and enunciates the principles manifest or latent in them. These are arguably the principles which should inform the decisions of all criminal courts. Sir Rupert Cross's *The English Sentencing System* (1975, 1981) also offers a set of generally understood principles of sentencing. Fallon (1975) and McLean (1980) both analyse sentencing practice from their position as serving members of the judiciary. More recently Ashworth (1983) sets principles of sentencing in the context of penal policy generally. Ashworth is critical of the arrogation to themselves by judges of penal policy decisions, and of the tenuousness of the influence of the Court of Appeal on sentencing decisions made lower in the system.

The literature on sentencing, the most notable contributions to which are mentioned above, is more modest than one would like. This may reflect the low importance which practising lawyers attach to sentencing. It may also reflect the speed with which a court typically arrives at a sentencing decision in contrast to the much greater time taken to convict in a contested case. Lord Devlin (1979) even suggests that sentencing is usually easy. 'In the majority of cases, there is little room for choice.' Yet sentencing principles seem to give enormous scope for choice. For example, in his description of tariff sentencing (i.e. sentencing based primarily on the seriousness of the offence) Thomas (1979a) gives a flavour of the tone of the literature. 'A tariff sentence will normally be upheld, without regard to the problems and needs of the offender, for a wide range of offences, *in some cases* with a degree of consistency which suggests a firm policy' (emphasis added). This implies substantial inconsistency, which may be the result of the disparate sentences of a large number of judges who see themselves as having 'little room for choice'.

Why should we not take the legal literature as it stands? Why not accept the principles which the academic lawyers infer from the reasoning of senior judges? The first answer to that question has little to do with psychology. It is that the (perforce) abstract and diffuse enunciation of sentencing principles offers limited scope for under-standing sentencing in the individual case. To the idiosyncratic sentencer the principles may represent a repertoire of usable justifi-cations of sentence. They offer little prospect of control over his idiosyncrasy. Nor do they present much opportunity for identifying him as idiosyncratic. David Thomas makes a fundamental distinction between tariff sentences, based on offence characteristics, and indi-vidualised sentences, based on offender characteristics. The range of application of the two sentencing modes is specified only in the broadest terms. In accepting such a distinction, different sentences in the same circumstances, and the same sentence in different circum-stances, can be justified merely by reference to different sentencing principles.

A second reason for scepticism about judges' expressions of sentencing principles does derive from the work of psychologists. The literature of cognitive psychology has shown, clearly and repeatedly, that people in general simply do not have enough access to their own thought processes for us to take their reasons seriously. The evidence for this strange and subversive claim will be touched on immediately and set out more fully in Chapter 3.

The mystique of decisions

Wilkins *et al.* (1972) describe the decision-making process as a one-way screen.

When we are looking towards it we know without any doubt that we have not passed through it, but when we look backwards, while we know we have passed through, the time, method or occasion of 'passing through' usually avoids us ... The linguistic conventions by which we describe the uncertainty we have before 'deciding' ... 'I have not yet made up my mind' (a construction analogy), 'I am still in doubt' (a locational analogy) ... 'I do not know which side to come down on' ... There is, perhaps, as rich a selection of phrases in which we can indicate that we have decided ... 'I have made up my mind', 'On balance I would say' and so on ... But consider the process of the act and deciding. We have no such phrases which refer to the decision-making operation.

In their analysis of problem-solving in civil law, Crombag *et al.* (1975) tried to elicit accounts from skilled problem-solvers. They concluded:

While skilled problem-solvers may not be able to tell us explicitly how they proceed while solving a problem, they are able to complete the solving itself. If we ask them to think aloud while solving a concrete problem and if we keep a record of this thinking aloud in written protocols, the analysis of the protocols might lead us to a formal description of what, in fact, is done. We have tried this, rather informally, but the results were disappointing. The most striking result was that what was said while thinking aloud created a rather chaotic and unsystematic impression. Often a person seemed to have a solution, although a provisional one, at an early stage, for which he subsequently tried to find supporting arguments. Moreover, during the reasoning process, the subject did not seem to complete one part after the other, but rather to jump wildly back and forth.

In interviews with Crown Court judges (Fitzmaurice, 1981), one judge mused thus: 'When a judge passes sentence ... there are so many things which he has got to take into account ... it's just in what I call the mental mixer of sentencing.' This sort of description is echoed by judges interviewed by Ashworth *et al.* (1984): 'Most judges described it as an instinctive process, using such terms as "instinct", "experience", "hunch" and "feeling".' In the authoritative *Encyclopaedia of Crime and Justice*, edited by Stanford Kadish (1983), Judge Marvin Aspen describes sentencing thus:

Sentencing is anything but a simple task. Many diverse data must be considered by the judge: other material must be consciously excluded from the sentencing equation. After this tortuous process, the judge will render a reasoned sentence that is subject to one final 'litmus' test: is the sentence what is best for society? If it is, then the judge has performed well.

It is the instinctive mental mixer's description of its own mode of operation that has provided much of the data for the development of principles of sentencing. It can be argued that a reconstruction of the sentencing process (in the form of giving reasons for sentence) is necessary in the cause of justice (Wilkins, 1984). What is argued here and will be argued more fully in Chapter 3 is that the giving of reasons for sentence may be a good idea, but, if so, it is not because the reasons thus generated are the real reasons for passing sentence, or are credible as the reasons. It is because the giving of reasons may reveal the sentences as *defensible* in terms of a principle or set of principles. It is remarkable that, in their reconstruction of complex mental events which they have experienced, people can take themselves seriously, be taken seriously by others, be confident and inspire confidence, and even deny the complexity of those events (see, for example, Devlin, 1979, on sentencing). The evidence, which will be reviewed later, makes it clear that the ability to reconstruct mental processes accurately is limited, occurring only when certain criteria are fulfilled, which are not fulfilled by the situations in which judicial sentencing takes place. This means, in short, that we either have to believe that judges are superhuman and that our understanding is satisfactory (in the same way that God's superiority makes him ineffable and consequently makes theology necessarily imperfect), or alternatively that judges share the cognitive frailties of other people, in which case research into the principles of sentencing must be put on a sounder footing, or based less on judicial accounts. Given judicial power, and given the opacity of the mental processes underpinning sentence, the practice of judicial sentencing demands scrutiny from all concerned citizens, not least the professional psychologist.

Psychologists as handmaidens of the powerful

Psychology has tended to be a conservative discipline. One of the problems linked to the issue of power in psychology has been that the *rapport de force* is not always obvious. Sometimes it is. Durndell (1977) notes, 'Psychology as a whole is not necessarily oriented towards the *status quo*, but it has a strong tendency to be so, particularly because of the pressures that employers of psychologists are

6 The psychology of judicial sentencing

liable to put on them in guiding research areas and techniques which are to be used towards the ends the employers desire.' Even when this is not so, there is a tendency to be conservative. Explanations given of psychological phenomena can themselves be the product of the respect for power. To give a famous example, we turn to one of the best known psychological principles, that of the Oedipus complex, taken by Freud (1922) from events described in Sophocles' play, *Oedipus Rex*. Oedipus kills his father, Laius, Freud argues, because of a jealous wish to possess his mother. In Sophocles' play, however, Laius is largely instrumental in causing his own death. He goads (in both senses) Oedipus, who retaliates with fatal results. Thus, in large measure, Laius' death resulted from his own bellicosity. Despite this, Freud takes the story as an illustration of the son's desire to kill the father. Popular culture as well as academic psychology has uncritically followed the conventional Freudian interpretation. Yet the conventional view fits the original story less well than does the alternative interpretation that the Oedipus myth is (if it is interpretable at all in terms of an understanding of the human condition) really about paternal envy and fear. Laius envied and feared the burgeoning strength and sensuality of his son, trying to kill or injure him with a two-pronged goad. The reader is invited to consider what Freud would have made of the two-pronged goad if Sophocles had placed it in Oedipus' rather than Laius' hands!

What has this got to do with the assertion that psychologists' interpretations can be the product of a respect for power? Fathers are more powerful than sons (physically until the son's adulthood, socially typically until the father's dotage). Unconscious wishes are more safely located in the psyches of sons than of fathers. Unconscious hostility is more safely located in the psyche of Oedipus than in that of Laius. What is meant by safety in this context? Safety here means the confidence of not suffering guilt or ridicule, the confidence that the blessings of the powerful will continue to be poured on the heads of those whose interpretations are acceptable to the powerful, unstemmed by the malicious biting of the powerful feeding hand. Consistent with this sort of interpretation is the fact that psychological research on decision-making in courts has tended to concentrate more on the decisions of jurors than on the decisions of judges (see Farrington and Hawkins, 1978). Perhaps judicial criticism of jurors by judges (see, for example, Baldwin and McConville, 1980) has been more likely to be translated into funded research than has jurors' criticism of judges. It is no coincidence that we are unable to cite a reference for criticism in this direction, whereas we had to select a reference for criticism in the other direction from among many alternatives.

In so far as judges have been the subject of study, work has tended to concentrate more on alleged judicial idiosyncrasies than on common standards capable of application to judicial performance (for a recent exception, see Ashworth *et al.*, 1984). For example, Hogarth (1971), Hagan (1974) and Chiricos and Waldo (1975) were largely concerned with differences among sentencers in the philosophy and attitudes which they brought to bear on the sentencing task, and the relationship of those differences to judicial performance or principles of judicial performance. Such an approach is a valuable one in addressing the problem of unwarranted sentencing variation. However, it necessarily takes the average of current judicial performance or current sentencing principles as unproblematic. It is thus less threatening to the general run of sentencing practice than would be, for example, an examination of the scaling of offence against punishment, or a challenge to the assumption of the capacity knowingly to tell the truth about the principles underlying one's own performance as a sentencer.

Some judges regard the process of sentencing as uncomplicated. In the opinion of Lord Devlin, 'In the majority of cases there is little room for choice. The judge has only to fix the appropriate term of imprisonment by applying the tariff to the circumstances of the case.' Yet an article in the *Sunday Times* (Knightley, 1982) described how research at the Oxford University Centre for Criminological Research 'to examine from a judge's point of view how the sentencing process worked' had been 'blocked' by the judiciary. The Lord Chief Justice is reported to have told the distinguished leaders of the project that 'research would not tell judges anything they did not already know, and that they were not prepared to co-operate'. If this is an accurate record of the Lord Chief Justice's remarks, and a correct reading by him of the feelings of the judiciary generally, then even the most obviously relevant and well-founded research, conducted by those best equipped for the job, is not seen as capable of improving judges' understanding of what they do and their capacity to do it.

This is a profoundly depressing state of affairs. It seems important to establish that there are areas of judicial performance which can be illuminated by psychological research, if not on judges themselves, then on others, where the behaviour studied has obvious parallels with sentencing. It will be a long and slow process to establish the relevance of the work with judges who are perhaps not always appropriately modest in their estimation of their capacity to sentence correctly. It is of no little interest that reference to the training of judges was removed from the title of the Bridge Committee, which eventually reported as the 'Working Party on Judicial Studies and Information' (1978).

Psychologists and judges

Two psychologists writing a book on the psychology of judicial sentencing must believe that the discipline has something to offer in this area. We do. Our view is not universal. King (1984) objects to approaches involving simulation studies, small samples, methods of analysis appropriate only to the natural sciences; more profoundly, 'unlike sociologists, [psychologists] have not, unfortunately, developed the theoretical models or methods of critical analysis which would enable and entitle them to apply psychological knowledge to the operations of social systems or even to identify the forces operating within these systems'. While not wishing to minimise the limitations of a psychological approach, and recognising Michael King as a scholar and practitioner whose views are worthy of great respect, we would nonetheless argue that the criteria of objectivity, replicability and falsifiability are substantial enough to confer some merit on the psychologist's enterprise. As for the more basic criticism, we have tried not to be unappreciative of the judicial task, but rather to bring to bear some ways of thinking about the behaviour in question. Both of us come from an empirical tradition in experimental psychology and value the characteristics of that approach. But the approach is, and must be, flexible enough to take into account the particular difficulties of the situation on which it is brought to bear. Our aim has been to clarify some of the problems raised by sentencing as it is now practised and to relate various aspects of the sentencing task to what we know from psychological research. At times the research was undertaken to shed light on human behaviour generally. In other cases the literature is a reflection of research aimed directly at sentencers. Regardless of the origins of the work, we see the purpose of the book as heuristic, not prescriptive. There are three themes:

(1) The discussion of psychological research applicable to the judicial task of sentencing.
(2) The description of a way of thinking about sentencing derived from psychological theory which suggests possibilities for understanding, monitoring and controlling judicial sentencing.
(3) The approach to some recognisable criminal justice system problems by psychologists.

The three themes merge into each other but appear in roughly that order. We have written for the lawyer rather than the psychologist, but we hope both will find something of interest in what follows.

Who guards the judges?

In the choice of material for inclusion, we have been guided by beliefs about and attitudes towards judicial performance. Some of these we are only now able to recognise. We shall describe, briefly and in broad terms, what we regard as judicial ideals towards which to strive. Psychology has developed according to two traditions, known as nomothetic and ideographic. For the nomothetic tradition, understanding of general principles of behaviour was sought. In the ideographic tradition, understanding of individual differences was the goal. Concerning sentencing, we discern two central questions to which the two traditions may respectively be addressed. They are:

(1) Is the judiciary deciding on principles of sentencing or on departures from such principles by means which are subject to kinds of error identifiable as those to which people generally are subject?
(2) Are sentencing decisions subject to unwarrantedly wide or narrow variation?

In our ideal judiciary, the answer to both questions would (obviously) be no. A case could be advanced (to which we would not subscribe) that if the answer to the first question were no, the answer to the second must also be no. Perhaps in consequence most of the book deals with the first question. It is certainly the more fundamental problem. Capricious decision-making is in principle much easier to correct than is uniform − and uniformly misconceived − decision-making. The devices for regulating sentencing disparity to be described in the next section of this chapter would be useless without examination of the issues raised by the first question. Convergence on a wrong answer has little merit.

Sentencing disparity

Differences in the use of punishments are easy to find. Disparities are difficult to demonstrate. Disparities exist, to put it at its most general, when similar offences, committed by people who are similar in relevant respects, receive different sentences. Differences in the use of punishment occur across epochs, between places and between cases dealt with in the same place at the same time. Differences in the use of punishment between epochs and between nations or regions tend not to excite a sense of injustice. They are not perceived as disparities and attempts to demonstrate that they are disparities tend not to be undertaken. In one trivial sense, differences over time which occur because of changes in sentences available are *ipso facto* disparities. The same is true of differences occurring by virtue of national or regional differences in sentence availability. Nonetheless, neither geographical nor historical changes in punishment use are seen as things to get greatly excited about. A sense of injustice is felt keenly only when sentences can be contrasted with other sentences passed at around the same time and in roughly the same place.

It is in these circumstances that the effort to identify differences as disparities has been made. Social class (Griffith, 1977) and political allegiance (Nagel, 1962) correlates of judicial behaviour have been sought and it is implausible to suppose that judicial value systems are irrelevant to sentencing. As Nagel argues, 'There probably will always be a residue of party-correlated judicial subjectivity as long as political parties are at least partly value-oriented and so long as court cases involve value-oriented controversies.' Indeed McKnight (1981) undertook a neat analysis of magisterial sentencing practice and demonstrated the predictability of sentences from values and the salience of values to individual cases. Hogarth's (1971) major work may be seen as lying in the same research tradition, as in England is that of Lemon (1974) and Hood's (1962) demonstration of the complex of variables associated with magistrates' sentencing, which showed that, for example, middle-class magistrates in small and stable middle-class communities imposed relatively severe sentences on working-class offenders. Cook (1973) showed that judges with draft-age sons dealt differently with draft evaders. One should not be surprised that a complex of factors including judicial socialisation, community pressures, pre-existing attitudes and personality affect sentencing (Champagne and Nagel, 1982) but it is surely misguided to analyse (in one study – Lasswell, 1948 – actually to psychoanalyse) judicial personality. No one could or should exclude judges from appointment on the basis of their personality (short of barking madness). The more proper approach must be to look for an association between extra-legal variables and sentence, and to seek to eliminate that influence, rather than to eliminate judges on the basis of personality-based predictions of their susceptibility to that influence.

American studies have tended to concentrate on offender race and social class as variables of interest in examining for the systematic effects of extra-legal variables on sentence. Some evidence exists of social class being at least associated with sentence severity, but the issue is finely balanced, with some commentators arguing that the data are inconclusive (Hagan, 1974; Chiricos and Waldo, 1975) and others that social class is an extra-legal variable with a clear link to sentence severity (Chambliss and Seidman, 1971; Jankovic, 1978). As for race, the evidence is rather stronger that blacks receive harsher sentences than whites in at least some of the United States (Lizotte, 1978; Stecher and Sparks, 1982), and on at least first offenders in New Zealand (Mugford and Gronfors, 1978). A third extra-legal variable which has attracted some recent attention is the attractiveness of the defendant, which leads to more lenient sentencing except where the attractiveness enabled the offence, as in frauds on men perpetrated by attractive women (Gray and Ashmore, 1976; Leventhal and Krate, 1977; Stewart, 1980; Diamond and Herhold, 1981). Interestingly, three recent British studies tend to exculpate courts from sentence bias; by race (McConville and Baldwin, 1982; Crow and Cove, 1984), by sex (Farrington and Morris, 1983) and by race and age of offender and race of victim (Kapardis and Farrington, 1981). More accurately, these studies fail to detect major bias on the lines looked for. Lest complacency be the response, there is enough room for disparity by race or sex earlier in the process to make the criminal justice system profoundly discriminatory, but as far as the meagre data go, this does not seem to operate in sentencing.

Discussion of sentencing disparity recalls controversies in the early years of psychology in which the resolution of fundamental issues turned on apparently minor details of method. In the same way, there has been a danger of the debate descending into a methodological morass. Certainly, no major challenge to sentencing practice could conceivably be mounted on the basis of early studies of disparity. Fortunately, it is reasonable to argue that one does not need to define disparity closely for the application of measures to reduce capricious decision-making. Wilkins (1980) argues that the sentencer has, implicitly, a set of variables in terms of which he considers it proper to adjust sentence. Disparity will be claimed in so far as the checklist of the claimant departs from the checklist of the sentencer. Thus Wilkins argues,

we cannot measure 'disparity' nor is it possible to define it without the likelihood of a dispute about some of its elements. Nonetheless, there is little doubt that there is such a factor, and it does require our attention. But that does not mean that it is necessary to measure it in any precise form ... 'Something' was there, but just like the accounts of blind men and the mythical elephant, it is difficult to describe precisely. If it were possible to design a system which provided a structure for the exercise of discretion, we thought that the problem would thereby be attended to.

Notwithstanding Wilkins' assertion, one can reasonably infer un-warranted sentence variation from those studies in which the same sentencers receive information on the same case and sentence differ-ently (see Partridge and Eldridge, 1974, cited in Saks and Hastie, 1978).

Such difference is also acknowledged by Judge King Hamilton (1982), who describes sentencing as 'either very easy or very difficult'. He argues that at the extremes it is very easy, but 'the difficulty comes in the very large grey area in between, when a dozen judges might give as many different sentences'. He describes one case: 'The luncheon adjournment came before the time to pass sentence. At lunch, I asked my brother judges for their advice. There were nine of us. I received eight different opinions.' While remaining unsure of what Judge King Hamilton means by different, the assertion of judicial disparity in sentencing could scarcely be more forcefully made. Ashworth *et al.* (1984) notes that 'although few judges stated that they personally felt a need for more guidance on sentencing levels, a number of judges thought it would be useful to *other* judges'. They further argue that a priority for further research is 'how it is that judges sometimes feel they have no alternative but to pass a particular sentence, when other judges would pass different sentences'.

The system which Wilkins evolved was that of sentencing guidelines.

To give an account of guideline development which would do justice to its innovativeness and ingenuity is beyond the scope of this book, and the reader is referred to Gottfredson and Gottfredson (1980), Kress (1980) and Wilkins (1980). In essence, the guidelines approach provides a system requiring the justification of atypical decisions, atypicality being defined by comparison with the set of cases which are similar in central respects adjudicated by all sentencers in the jurisdiction area, not merely the sentencer of the offender in any particular case. Central respects are defined empirically as those accounting for the bulk of the variance in sentencing decisions generally, namely offence gravity and prior record (in practice, the 'salient factor score' is rather wider than simple prior record, but the notion of criminal history includes all the facts from which the salient factor score is compiled). See Hoffman and Adelberg (1980) for a detailed account of the salient factor score and van Dijk (1983) for equivalent Dutch data. Taking these two variables, a matrix is generated on the basis of previous sentencing practice. Each cell of the matrix contains the middle range of sentences for offences of that seriousness committed by offenders with that salient factor score. Middle range may be the middle 80 per cent of sentences, excluding the most severe 10 per cent and the least severe 10 per cent. Table 1 reproduces two sample U.S. guidelines. (The distinction between felonies and misdemeanours was abolished in English law in 1967.) To illustrate the operation, for the upper set of guidelines, an offence of seriousness score 6, committed by an offender with a salient factor score of 7, would yield a guideline range of 16–20 months' incarceration. If a sentencer wished to pass a sentence outside that range, reasons must be given, which reasons are appealable. Hopefully, it will be clear to the reader that the 'out' description means that the middle range of sentences are all non-custodial. The analogy of the guidelines with a road mileage chart is overworked because it is so appropriate.

The guidelines approach ensures that the justification for very atypical sentences are made available for inspection and appeal. It means that the subset of atypical sentences which are indeed capricious have a chance of being identified as such and overturned. However, the choice of a middle way between unfettered discretion and mandatory sentencing makes the guidelines movement vulnerable to a number of criticisms. Perhaps the most important is that basing guidelines on existing judicial practice may smuggle into the process the effects of the same extra-legal variables which affected sentencing before guidelines (and many of the factors described in Chapter 2, although none of these has been identified in criticisms of guidelines up to now). For example, in so far as race has been a factor in sentencing practice, guidelines ignoring the race factor will, relative to previous practice, be excessively severe for whites and lenient for blacks. Stecher and Sparks (1982) have shown interactions between race and the guideline variables in determining sentence. They conclude, 'In this case, unless race is explicitly included in the model, the effect of that relevant factor may be misestimated. Exclusion of race and other such factors from modelling equations may thus build into the subsequently created guidelines the very kinds of things that guidelines are supposed to avoid.' This is a particular example of the general point that guidelines may be seen to be evidence-derived rather than policy-derived i.e. descriptive rather than prescriptive. Galligan (1981) makes a linked observation, that presumptive sentences are averaged across cases dealt with according to different principles, and are thus inappropriate for those dealt with according to any particular sentencing principle. it is unlikely that the advocates of guidelines would dissent, but they would regard these differences in sentence according to underlying principles as constituting unwarranted variation, a view which Galligan clearly does not share.

Nonetheless, the major point stands, namely that unless the social policy implications of all the empirically based choices made are fully recognised, guidelines will contain unrecognised policy. The developers of the guidelines should be exempted from any criticism that they were unaware of this. They were obviously and unremittingly at pains to explicate the policy implications of choices that were made. One remains unconvinced that all the choice implications were recognised. For example the choice of a broad (80 per cent) rather than a narrow (perhaps 40 per cent) range is a statement about the appropriate band of indifference to sentence choice. The danger of broad widths is that enough discretionary power is thereby provided for large amounts of unchallenged caprice to remain. Certainly the existence of guidelines in no way removes or diminishes the need for an analysis of sentencing of the kind advocated in Chapter 6, although it may be perceived to do so. Wasik (1982) identifies other guideline difficulties involved in sentencing for conspiracy, and in the coexistence of guidelines and mandatory minimum sentences. Related difficulties are mentioned in Forst (1982) and Sparks (1983). A possible

Table 1 *Examples of the dispositions indicated by guidelines: two categories of offence type*

Misdemeanour 1[a]

		Offender Score			
		−1	0	6	9
		−7	5	8	11	12+
Offence score	10−12	18−24 months	18−24 months	18−24 months	18−24 months	18−24 months
	8−9	Out	Out	18−24 months	18−24 months	18−24 months
	6−7	Out	Out	16−20 months	18−24 months	18−24 months
	3−5	Out	Out	Out	8−10 months	12−15 months
	1−2	Out	Out	Out	Out	9−12 months

Felony 5[b]

		Offender Score			
		−1	0	4	8
		−7	3	7	11	12+
Offence score	10−12	Indet. Min. 4−5 year max.	Indet. Min. 4−5 year max.	Indet. Min. 4−5 year max.	Indet. Min. 4−5 year max.	Indet. Min. 4−5 year max.
	8−9	Out	Out	Indet. Min. 3−4 year max.	Indet. Min. 3−4 year max.	Indet. Min. 4−5 year max.
	6−7	Out	Out	Out	Indet. Min. 3−4 year max.	Indet. Min. 4−5 year max.
	3−5	Out	Out	Out 2−3 year max.	Indet. Min. 4−5 year max.	Indet. Min.
	1−2	Out	Out	Out	Out	Indet. Min. 4−5 year max.

Notes

(a) The statutory designated minimum incarcerative sentence for a misdemeanour 1 offence is 6 months. The maximum is 24 months. A definite term of incarceration is generally set by the court.

(b) The statutory designated maximum incarcerative sentence for a felony 5 offence is 5 years. No minimum period of confinement is to be set by the court.

difficulty is that flowing from a study of perceptual anchoring, from which one would predict that the guidelines would reduce the number of sentences outside the presumptive range by acting as an anchor. Finally, the important possibility must be made explicit that while the guidelines limit sentencing discretion, discretion elsewhere in the system may be used differently, for example, in the choice of charge and in plea-bargaining.

Notwithstanding all the criticisms which may be levelled against the guidelines movement, guidelines place the analysis of sentencing differences on an entirely new footing, one in which it is possible to be optimistic that it may proceed in ways which directly inform sentencing practice. Guidelines at least provide decision-makers, both sentencers and other penal policy-makers, with usable information. It structures not only discretion, but the debate about discretion's use. Given the historical impotence of social science in criminal justice, that is no small achievement.

CHAPTER 2

Cognitive errors and judges

It is very recently that cognitive psychology has made a serious attempt to stop being patronising about practical decision-makers. Judges have by and large not yet stopped being patronising about psychologists. The story is told by Professor L. R. C. Haward of his giving evidence to a court about the extremely low tested IQ of a defendant, the inference being that he could not have carried out the crime, the commission of which involved some sophistication. Professor Haward reports the judge's intervention to ask, 'If a Fellow of the Royal Society had obtained a similar score on this test, would you have concluded that he was of low intelligence?' Professor Haward replied, yes, that is what he would have concluded. The judge thereupon delivered himself of the view that 'If the test leads one to suppose that a Fellow of the Royal Society is of extremely low intelligence, I think we can tell what sort of a test that is.' This is no doubt an extreme example, but it is difficult to conclude that the spirit which gave it birth is uncommon.

If, then, cognitive psychology has not addressed itself to the problems of sentencing, and if sentencers have not sought to inform themselves about cognitive psychology, what can be written? Hopefully, a good deal, since many examples of difficulties in decision-making have been revealed and clarified by cognitive psychology which are clearly analogous to the kinds of difficulty which sentencers face. In this chapter we review certain commonly observed cognitive errors. Its tone is tentative, the object being to connect with judicial sentencing a literature which we regard as centrally relevant to it — an exercise which, to our knowledge, has not previously been attempted. The working assumption is that the errors to be described manifest themselves in judicial sentencing no less than elsewhere in human behaviour, but the direct demonstration of their relevance should be undertaken. Until it is, our presumption is that judges reason and act like everyone else.

In what follows, discussion of each of the judgment errors will contain three elements: a brief description of the nature of the error, some account of the experimental evidence for the existence of the error, and speculation about the effects of the error on judicial performance.

The fundamental attribution error

People underestimate the impact of situational factors and over-estimate the role of dispositional factors in controlling behaviour. Evidence for this comes from the general finding that what is said or done, even when it is obviously done on request or demand, is taken as an indication of the person's real inclinations more than it should (see, e.g. Jones and Harris, 1967). Additionally, inference about a person's ability similarly ignores situational evidence. A particularly neat demonstration of the neglect of situational information comes from a study by Ross, Amabile and Steinmetz (1977). They set up a general-knowledge quiz game. One person was randomly assigned the role of questioner, another the role of contestant, a third the role of observer. The questioner had to compose a set of difficult general-knowledge questions, to ask the contestant the questions and to tell the contestant the right answer. Subsequently questioner, contestant and observer were asked to rate the questioner's and the contestant's general knowledge. Both contestant and observer in this situation consistently rated the questioner as superior to the contestant in general knowledge. Clearly this is an unjustified conclusion, because the situation allows the contestant opportunities to demonstrate his ignorance which are denied to the questioner, and allows the questioner opportunities to demonstrate his knowledge which are denied to the contestant. Nonetheless, the observers are willing to make the 'fundamental attribution error', by ascribing personal differences where the real differences are situational.

The effect of the fundamental attribution error in the courtroom would be for judges (and others) to attribute ineptitude to personal deficiencies rather than ignorance of situations. Specific to sentencing, the error would lead to insufficient account being taken of situational pressures when sentencing. 'Insufficient' would be difficult to quantify in any circumstances, and particularly difficult absent the tight control of experimentation. Nonetheless the suggestion is that where situational pressures are intense (offences committed as members of a large group, offences committed in times of need or other pressure) sentencers will exaggerate the extent to which people in general would have turned aside from the offence's commission. Ashworth *et al.* (1984) note of their sample of judges: 'Most ... believed that the factors which predominantly inhibit most people from committing crimes are moral beliefs and fear of social stigma', both personal rather than situational factors. In the same study, judges are held to subscribe to the view that 'The reason why there is a disproportionate number of persons from the lower socio-economic groups in prison is that they commit more crimes, and this was attributed by some judges to lower intelligence and lower moral standards among these groups.'

False consensus bias

People tend to generalise falsely from their own views to a belief in a consensus. They take their own choices and judgments to be relatively common and appropriate to existing circumstances while viewing alternative responses as uncommon, deviant and inappropriate. Put another way, one exaggerates the commonness of one's own behaviour and exaggerates the uncommonness of those who behave otherwise. A corollary of this links with the fundamental attribution error, namely that when someone is thought to behave differently from oneself, that behaviour is taken to reveal his personal characteristics. In contrast, one's own behaviour is a common-sense judgment based on the situation and (so the false consensus bias dictates) it is what most people agree on.

Evidence about the false consensus bias comes both from hypothetical conflict situations posed in questionnaires and from real-life conflict situations. In a study by Ross, Greene and House (1977) subjects read descriptions of situations they might face and were required to estimate the commonness of the two possible response alternatives, state which alternative they would follow and assess the characteristics of the 'typical' person who would follow each of the two specified alternatives. The study demonstrated false consensus in that people thought that the alternative they chose would be relatively more common than the unchosen alternative. Furthermore, people made more confident and more extreme inferences about the typical person who would perform the unchosen alternative. The same picture emerged from a real-life (?) study, where students were asked to walk round their college campus wearing a sandwich-board bearing the legend 'Eat at Joe's'. Those who agreed to do this thought more people would agree than did those who refused. Those who were willing to wear the board made more confident and extreme judgments of the characteristics of people who refused to wear it. Those who refused made more confident and extreme judgments about those who complied.

The false consensus bias is, it is argued, likely to be a central one in informing judicial sentencing practice. Wilkins (1983) recalls,

I once asked a judge whose opinions on sentencing commanded international respect, if he had ever made a wrong decision in sentencing. Unlike the judge who reported his infallibility to the Sunday Times, this judge argued that a mistake was possible. I then followed up with the question as to how he would distinguish an incorrect sentence decision. He replied that if nearly all the persons 'in the public gallery' thought that it was wrong, then it probably was.

The question is how such a judge would come to know the response of the public gallery, short of noisy outrage. In so far as judges rely on their own perception of consensus, they are bound to exaggerate the degree to which their sentences are acceptable. One wonders too about the extent to which the false consensus bias underlies judicial pronouncements like 'The ordinary Englishman is against reform'; 'The English judiciary is treated as a national institution, like the navy, and tends to be admired to excess'; and most remarkably:

Judges do lead the comfortable life of a successful professional man, and this is not the ordinary life. It is the sort of life led by many successful people, such as politicians, editors, writers of all sorts, and many kinds of merchants, whose job it is to know what ordinary people are thinking and how they are likely to react. The knowledge is obtained instinctively and independently of whether a man lives in a palace or a council house. (Devlin 1979)

Dare we suggest that Lord Devlin has fallen prey to the false consensus bias? An aspect of this is that he tends (not in the passage quoted) to dismiss rather easily scepticism of the judge's intuition of popular opinion. Ashworth *et al.* (1984) conclude: 'It seemed from our pilot study that most judges thought they were capable of identifying "informed public opinion" and that a majority believed that it coincided with their own opinions.' No judge in that study thought that there would be majority disagreement with their identification of 'especially heinous' offences. For the majority of judges who took the view that their social distance from defendants was not a problem, those who offered reasons stated, 'that they came from humble beginnings (all who gave this reason had attended public school) or that they lived ordinary lives.'

Anchoring effects

An anchor limits the range of movement of a ship. A perceptual anchor limits the range of a judgment. So supplying a starting-point (anchor) for consideration of an issue changes the range within which that judgment will be made.

Evidence for anchoring effects is easy to come by. Two examples from Tversky and Kahneman (1974) will be provided. Asked a question about the percentage of African countries in the United Nations, one group of people was given the starting point for estimation of 10 per cent and another the starting-point of 65 per cent. The final estimates of the two groups were 25 per cent and 45 per cent respectively. Rewarding people for the accuracy of their estimates did not help. Another technique, exhibiting an elegance of method for which Tversky and Kahneman are well known, involved getting students to estimate the product $8 \times 7 \times 6 \times 5 \times 4 \times 3 \times 2 \times 1$ within five seconds. Another group had to estimate the product $1 \times 2 \times 3 \times 4 \times 5 \times 6 \times 7 \times 8$ in the same time. The first group estimated the product at 2,250 and the second at 512. The anchor of what was read first was thus highly influential in determining the final product.

The anchoring effect is obviously of great importance in tariff sentencing. The notional sentence or sentence range specified by tariff sentencing principles will act as an anchor for sentence choice. Thus the existence of a well-understood common tariff will limit sentencing variation, by restricting the range from the notional tariff sentence which will be used. By the same token informal local tariffs (see Tarling, 1980) will increase sentencing variation by anchoring different local practices at different levels.

Anchoring also has interesting implications for the ways in which decisions of the Court of Appeal might operate on sentencing in lower courts. It has been argued (McLean, 1980) that levels of sentencing approved by the Court of Appeal are much higher than those typically imposed in the Crown Court. This is itself explicable in terms of an anchoring effect. Those sentences with which the Court of Appeal deals (on which it is anchored) are those which are regarded as arguably excessive. In so far as the judgments of Crown Courts are informed by (anchored on) Court of Appeal judgments, they will generally increase. There is only one protection against a *folie à deux* of the courts with a consequent sentencing spiral. This is the slightness of the extent to which the Crown Court is influenced by Court of Appeal decisions! The conclusion of this line of argument is that the introduction of a prosecution right of appeal would have the incidental effect of anchoring the Court of Appeal in a more diverse set of sentencing decisions, and would thereby bring Court of Appeal sentencing closer into line with Crown Court sentencing. At present, we would fear the consequences of a greater influence for Court of Appeal decisions, believing that it would create a progressive increase in the general level of sentencing.

Anchoring has particularly interesting implications for the use of sentencing guidelines (see Chapter 1). How national sentencing practices become anchored in different ways is a fascinating (we think) topic which is outside the scope of this book.

Insensitivity to prior probabilities

People tend to ignore or to underplay the prior probability of outcomes and to emphasise unduly individual case information in making decisions.

Kahneman and Tversky (1973) got people to perform one of three tasks. One was 'Consider all first-year graduate students in the US today. Please write down your best guesses about the percentage of these students who are enrolled in each of the following nine fields of specialisation.' Nine specialisms were then listed. A second task involved the presentation of the following personality sketch:

Tom W. is of high intelligence, although lacking in true creativity. He has a need for order and clarity, and for neat and tidy systems in which every detail finds its appropriate place. His writing is rather dull and mechanical, occasionally enhanced by somewhat corny puns and by flashes of imagination of the sci-fi type. He has a strong drive for competence. He seems to have little feel and little sympathy for other people and does not enjoy interacting with others. Self-centred, he nonetheless has a real moral sense.

When people had read this description, they were asked 'How similar is Tom W. to the typical graduate student in each of the following nine fields of graduate specialisation?', the nine fields being of course the same as for the first task. The last task of Kahneman and Tversky involved the presentation of the same personality sketch of Tom W. with the following additional information:

The preceding personality sketch of Tom W. was written during Tom's senior year in high school by a psychologist, on the basis of projective tests. Tom W. is currently a graduate student. Please rank the following nine fields of graduate specialisation in order of the likelihood that Tom W. is now a graduate student in each of these fields.

We should now go back slightly to consider what the different outcomes to this experiment would mean. There are two kinds of information which people could use to arrive at their estimate of the likelihood of Tom W. becoming a graduate student in a particular profession. The first is how many people become graduate students in each field. If, for example, it is twice as likely that someone becomes a graduate student in business administration than in medicine then, all other things being equal, it should be twice as likely that Tom W. should become a graduate student in business administration as in medicine. Even if all other things are not equal, then the difference is at least relevant in determining the likelihood of Tom's possible specialisation. What actually happened, however, was an almost complete reliance on Tom's similarity to the stereotype of different professions. Because he sounded like a computer scientist, he was thought to be likely to be training to be one. The base rate was effectively ignored, in favour of complete reliance on information about the individual case. This was so even though people did not regard the projective tests used to generate the individual information as accurate. In fact they regarded such tests as extremely inaccurate. Despite this, they ignored the base rate in favour of case information they recognised as highly fallible.

These amazing results mean that people ignored information about prior probabilities even when they knew the individual information to be misleading. Can it really be the case that people so much prefer to base their judgments on information about individuals that they will do so even when that information is fallible, and that in doing so they will ignore information about overall probabilities which they could properly use? In a series of experiments designed to test this possibility, Kahneman and Tversky's subjects continued to act with perverse indifference to prior probabilities. For example, people were told that a group consisted of seventy engineers and thirty lawyers, and Dick had been selected at random from that group of 100. They then were told that 'Dick is a thirty-year-old man. He is married with no children. A man of high ability and high motivation, he promises to be quite successful in his field. He is well liked by his colleagues.' Obviously this description is utterly uninformative with respect to the likelihood of Dick being a lawyer or an engineer. What do people guess as the probability of Dick being a lawyer? They estimate the likelihood to be 50 per cent. If told that a group consists of seventy lawyers and thirty engineers, people still say that the probability that Dick is a lawyer is 50 per cent. Does this mean that people are simply incapable of using prior probabilities in their estimates? The answer is no. If given no information about Dick at all, people will say that, in a group of which 70 per cent are lawyers, there is a 0·7 chance that Dick is a lawyer. Kahneman and Tversky's conclusion, which can properly be described as shattering, is that 'People respond differently when given no specific evidence and when given worthless evidence. When no specific evidence is given, the prior probabilities are properly used; when worthless specific evidence is given, prior probabilities are ignored.'

If this evidence can properly be generalised, it means that, in sentencing, information will be used about individual cases in preference to information about base rates, even when the individual information is worthless in determining probability of reconviction. For example, if the judge knows that seven out of ten people convicted of burglary are reconvicted within two years, but is impressed with the demeanour of a particular burglar in the dock, does he sentence on the basis of prior probability (seven chances in ten of reconviction) or in terms of the more hopeful individual judgment? The suggestion from Kahneman and Tversky is that he sentences on the basis of the individual data. Certainly it is the writers' experience that sentencers are unaware of, and if aware do not seek out, base data which are readily available to them.

Ashworth *et al.* (1984) also clearly show how central individual assessments are:

The observational research and the discussions with judges also suggested that the defendant's demeanour and 'attitude' in court were regarded as legitimate and indeed significant matters to be taken into account. The tendency of some judges to classify particular defendants within certain 'types', and the inferences drawn from courtroom behaviour to the defendant's attitude towards his offence, suggest that the personality of the judge may also in these respects shape his assessment of the 'facts of the case'.

Is there any more satisfactory evidence of the relevance of the insensitivity to prior probability in sentencing? Such evidence as exists is tenuous and indirect, but it will be rehearsed.

The grant or withholding of parole is not strictly a sentencing decision, although it unquestionably involves a considerable element of resentencing (see for example Hood, 1974). The reason why it is relevant here is the availability of a data base unrivalled in penal practice in the United Kingdom. This is the Parole Index. For every male determinate-sentence prisoner in England and Wales, the Parole Board is provided with a host of information, of which one element is the predicted probability of reconviction within two years of release (for details of how and why the Parole Index was developed, see Nuttall *et al.*, 1977). However, in the early days of parole in England and Wales, the relationship between probability of reconviction and chances of release on licence was very imperfect (Nuttall *et al.*, 1977). There is no more recent evidence about that relationship, although there are two indirectly relevant facts. First, it is the case that no member of the Parole Board to whom we have spoken regards the predicted probability of reconviction as information important to their function. Second, although probability of reconviction diminishes as sentence length increases, chances of release on licence also decline. Thus predicted probability of reconviction is, to put the case at its lowest, not so influential in determining release as to outweigh other factors.

A rather different observation about parole can be made, stemming from the fact that the calculation of predicted probability of reconviction has remained unaltered since 1967. Conversations with both officials and members of the Parole Board make it clear that what they are concerned with is not reconviction *per se*, but reconviction for serious, primarily violent, offences. It would be perfectly possible to recalculate the predicted probability of conviction score to make it specific to violent offences but, to our knowledge, no request that this should be done has ever been made by, or on behalf of, the Board. The most plausible reason for this is surely that information about prior probabilities is swamped by even the most meagre details of individual cases. This is certainly the sense of the process one gets from observation of the Parole Board.

It is always dangerous to argue from absence or omission. It can, however, be no coincidence that one of the least well known (outside the narrow circle of criminology) of the recent Home Office research studies is the one which provides detailed base rate information in a form which is usable by sentencers (Philpotts and Lancucki, 1979). The base rate information in the research appendix of the Home Office's guide for magistrates, 'The Sentence of the Court', was also almost universally ignored by magistrates. If the tendency to ignore usable base rate information exists among sentencers, they are not alone among decision-makers in the criminal justice system. Research by McWilliams (1975) among homeless male offenders showed clearly that probation officers were prepared to ignore well-founded information about their low probability of success with such offenders on the basis of the offender's individual characteristics. This is what Kahneman and Tversky would predict.

Misconceptions of regression

Statistical regression is the term given to the tendency for a measure which is extreme relative to other measures to be extreme relative to itself at other times. That somewhat opaque description will, it is hoped, become clearer after expansion. It is the most concise description of the effect, and it is hoped that the reader will find it comprehensible after the following development of the ideas underlying it. Imagine you wished to conduct trials of running speed among people in your town so as to select representatives for inter-town sports. It is likely that, on the day of the inter-town sports, your team members would on average run more slowly then they did during the trials (assuming that adrenalin was already running optimally high on the day of the trials). Why would they run more slowly? Assume the team contains five members, and the ten fastest runners in the town *all* have personal average times of say eleven seconds for the 100 metres. The five selected in the trials were obviously more 'on form' than the other five. What does 'on form' mean? It means that one is performing better than one usually does. If (in the trial) you perform better than you usually do, that means that when you do it again (in the event proper), you will usually do it worse! Thus, to restate, regression is the tendency for a measure which is extreme relative to other measures to be extreme relative to itself at other times.

What has regression got to do with sentencing? There are two answers. The first is related to the notion of crime waves and exemplary sentences. If a crime presents itself as a problem relative to itself at other times, its rate is more likely to go down than to go up. Therefore the imposition of exceptionally severe sentences at times when a crime is prevalent, followed by a decline in the rate of the crime, may lure the sentencer into the erroneous belief that the exemplary sentence produced the decline. There are only two directly relevant pieces of British evidence. The first (Baxter and Nuttall, 1975) showed that a sentence of twenty years' custody on a sixteen-year-old boy in 1973 had an apparent, but not a real, effect on the rate of muggings in Birmingham. Similarly a claim in 1965 by the Recorder of Birmingham that he had, by passing severe sentences, discouraged an outbreak of theft and damage in telephone kiosks, is not upheld by an analysis of data prepared by David Thomas and briefly reported in Walker (1980). (As a footnote, the effect of judicial pronouncements on public perceptions of crime now seems very trivial (Walker and Marsh, 1984).) Such research seems most unlikely to have dented judicial confidence. For example, Judge King-Hamilton (1982) opines 'sentences passed on the football fan hooligans who wreck trains, break shop windows, damage cars, carry offensive weapons and inflict serious bodily harm are far too lenient ... I make so bold as to suggest that these offences might be stopped virtually overnight by one or two really exemplary sentences.'

The second possible relevance of regression effects is cf a rather similar kind, but concerns crimes within a criminal career rather than across criminal careers. For example, consider an offender with two previous convictions for taking and driving away a motor vehicle, followed by one for assault causing grievous bodily harm. This last offence attracts a prison sentence which is followed by a further offence of taking and driving away a motor vehicle. There are (at least) two ways of 'reading' this criminal record. The first is to suggest that the prison sentence de-escalated the criminal career. The second interpretation is that the assault was atypical of the criminal career and was in any case likely to be followed by a more normal offence. This second is a regression interpretation. The tendency to interpret regression effects as real changes seems pretty general. It is attested not only by Kahneman and Tversky's research but also by the most cursory examination of political pronouncements. Any panic-based measure is likely to appear effective, because the circumstances which produced the panic are, almost by definition, extreme. Extreme circumstances, through regression, typically become less extreme. Campbell and Stanley (1966) invent the delightful 'trapped administrator' whose success he owes to the fact that he only acts when things are at their worst. The particularly interesting aspect of this, looked at in relation to judicial sentencing, is the spurious belief it might induce in the sentencer about the relationship between his sentencing and an offender's subsequent behaviour. Perhaps it would be best to introduce this point, which we believe to be important, indirectly through a consideration of one of Kahneman and Tversky's tasks. The reader is invited to go through the problem below and answer the question it poses before reading beyond it.

The instructors in a flight school adopted a policy of consistent positive reinforcement recommended by psychologists. They verbally reinforced each successful execution of a flight manoeuvre. After some experience with this training approach, the instructors claimed that, contrary to psychological doctrine, high praise for good execution of complex manoeuvres typically results in a decrement of performance on the next try. What should the psychologist say in response?

The reasons which graduate students in psychology gave for the effect were that verbal reinforcements might be ineffective for pilots or that they could lead to overconfidence. Some students doubted the validity of the impressions of the flight instructors. Of course the simple explanation for the effect is regression. As Kahneman and Tversky note, 'Regression is inevitable in flight manoeuvres because performance is not perfectly reliable and progress ... is slow. Hence, pilots who did exceptionally well on one trial are likely to deteriorate on the next, regardless of the instructor's reaction to the initial success.' More generally, by regression alone, behaviour will improve after harsh treatment and deteriorate after lenient treatment.

Applied directly and narrowly to the sentencing task, the regression effect would suggest that sentencers should develop greater confidence in the efficacy of harsh than of lenient sentences, with consequent temptation to increase the general level of sentences imposed. Fortunately for the humanity of our criminal justice system, a direct and narrow application of regression effects is not sensible. To take one reason among many, all those cases in which the sentencer is called upon to examine previous records are failures, varying only in the degree of seriousness of the failure. The impact of the regression effect depends upon the sentencer having no recollection of or views about what produced the real successes. This is clearly an area in which research is necessary. Depending on its outcome, an understanding of regression effects will either be essential in judicial training, or at worst a harmless diversion. The suspicion that it may be of importance is the finding of Tversky and Kahneman (1973) that cases which are more retrievable to memory will also be judged more frequent. Specifically in their experiment they found that when they presented lists comprised of the names of, for example, ten famous men and ten less famous women, people think there are more men's names in the list. When the women named are more famous, the opposite happens. It is at least arguable then that cases in which there has been a reconviction will be more retrievable in memory and will exert a disproportionate influence on guesses as to the effects of sentence on reconviction. If this speculation is true, it may serve to persuade judges that more severe sentences than those leading to reconvictions should be imposed, and exacerbates the tendency identified by Ashworth (1983) to punish persistence.

Illusory correlation

When variables are believed to be related to each other, they will be seen to be related even when they are not. Chapman and Chapman (1971) used the 'Draw a Person' test in which someone is simply given a pencil and a blank sheet of paper and is asked to draw a person. This projective test, developed in 1949, purports to show relationships between features of the person drawn and personality characteristics of the person drawing. For example its begetter Machover claimed that the paranoid individual gives much graphic emphasis to the eyes, and that the size of head is related to attributes of intellectual and social authority. Generally subsequent research has shown that these 'signs' are invalid. Chapman and Chapman 'gathered 45 drawings of male figures, 35 by psychotic patients at a nearby state hospital and 10 by graduate students in clinical psychology. We measured each picture for head size, eye size etc. and had independent judges rate the drawings on the more subjective characteristics, such as masculinity and femininity.' They then made up six diagnostic statements, like 'The man who drew this is worried about how intelligent he is', 'The man who drew this had problems of sexual impotence.' The descriptions were allocated to drawings such that in reality there was *no* relationship between characteristics of the drawing and diagnostic statements. For example drawings of small heads appeared as often as drawings of large heads alongside the diagnostic statement 'The man who drew this is worried about how intelligent he is.' Despite this complete absence of any real relationship, people persistently 'saw' that large heads had been drawn by people worried about their intelligence, broad shoulders had been drawn by people worried about their manliness, atypical eyes were drawn by people with paranoid feelings. This quite illusory perception of the 'common-sense' relationship was very resistant to change, and persisted even when there was a high incentive for accuracy and when the picture–statement pairings were rigged so that they actually showed the opposite of what they were perceived to show.

The implications for sentencing of the illusory correlation are troubling. Feedback of results is a necessary condition of learning anything, and judges are and remain in ignorance of the specific consequences of their sentencing practice. However, the illusory correlation means that to a large extent people insulate themselves against the recognition that treasured (or common-sense) relationships which are perceived to exist do not in fact exist. The resistance to change which the illusory correlations of Chapman and Chapman exhibited, if also shown by sentencers, means that sentencers may in all conscience believe that, for example, the detention centre decreases the probability of reconviction and that probation is particularly suitable for women, by no strategy more complex than simply underestimating the proportion of women given probation (or people given detention centre orders) who reappear before the court.

One of the mechanisms through which this misperception might occur may be illustrated in a study by Wason (1960) which the reader is invited to repeat on friends (particularly on friends who are judges). Wason showed people a three-number sequence, for example, 4, 6, 8. People were asked to discover the rule which Wason had in mind and to which the sequence conformed. The rule was of three numbers in ascending order. To discover the rule, people were permitted to generate sets of three numbers which, in each case, Wason reported to them as conforming or not conforming to the rule. People could stop at any time and tell Wason what they thought the rule was. The correct approach to this problem involves a search for counter evidence. For example if someone believed that the rule was something to do with increases by two, he would have to generate series in which the numbers changed by something other than two. Any number of series in which the increase was two would not test the rule. Yet most of the people studied by Wason kept generating series in which the numbers increased by two. Only six of his twenty-nine subjects found the correct rule the first time they thought they had. Wason's subjects behaved as though they could arrive at the rule by continuing to generate positive instances of what they thought the rule was.

Wason's study is by no means the only demonstration of the hypnotic power of positive instances. Jenkins and Ward (1965), Smedslund (1963, 1966) and Ward and Jenkins (1965) have all shown that people judge the strength of relationship by the number of positive hits, ignoring the other three kinds of relevant case. To concretise this error, let us return to the case of women given probation which we discussed earlier. Four categories of case are relevant to a decision about the idea that women given probation are reconvicted less. They are:

(1) Women given probation who are not reconvicted.
(2) Women given probation who are reconvicted.
(3) Women given a sentence other than probation who are reconvicted.
(4) Women given a sentence other than probation who are not reconvicted.

The evidence is that, if they behave like other people, judges will overestimate the relevance of the first category of case at the expense of the other three in reaching conclusions about the relationship between probation and reconviction. (In the debate about offender dangerousness, it seems that the heat of the argument owes much to differences in emphasis of the four possible types of case by those who take opposing positions on the merits of preventive custody for those classed as dangerous.)

Returning finally to Wason's study cited earlier, it is significant to recall Einhorn's (1980) observation that 'in Wason's experiment, where actions were not involved, a search for evidence is possible. However, when actions are based on judgement, learning based on counter evidence becomes more difficult to achieve.' In our example, once a sentencer is persuaded that women benefit from probation, feedback from other sentences on women is likely to be less available because women will have been put on probation. This elimination of feedback possibilities operates spectacularly in the case of parole, where the decision to deny parole to a particular class of case precludes the feedback one would get from behaviour on licence.

The knew-it-all-along effect

The knew-it-all-along effect is the affliction to which people are subject by exaggerating with hindsight what they could have predicted with foresight. The relevant research (Fischhoff, 1975, 1977; Fischhoff and Beyth, 1975; Wood, 1978) typically presents people with descriptions of a sequence of events with and without a dénouement. The probability of the known outcome is seen as more probable with hindsight than it had been without hindsight. More strikingly, people even misremember their own predictions so as to exaggerate with hindsight what they knew with foresight. As Fischhoff (1980) concludes:

When we attempt to understand past events, we implicitly test the hypotheses or rules we use both to interpret and to anticipate the world around us. If, in hindsight, we systematically underestimate the surprises that the past held and holds for us, we are subjecting those hypotheses to inordinately weak tests and presumably finding little reason to change them. Thus the very outcome knowledge which gives us the feeling that we understand what the past was all about may prevent us from learning anything about it.

One example of the possible application of the knew-it-all-along effect is that a judge may, when sentencing someone with a previous record, reconstruct with inappropriate confidence the likelihood of the reappearance before the court, and may reconstruct a story about what explained the reappearance. It is argued that the effect of this would be to increase the severity of sentence imposed on those with previous records beyond the increase which would be appropriate on other grounds (although a hard-line retributivist would argue that no increase in sentence on the basis of prior record can be justified).

Another example, adapted from Wood (1978), suggests that if a parolee commits a murder, those who authorised release on parole will have their decision second-guessed by people who will conclude that they knew what the outcome would be all along. One may also speculate that because of the knew-it-all-along effect and the fundamental attribution error mentioned earlier, the reasonable-man criterion in legal decisions will give results which are systematically unfair to a defendant, since what is knowable to a reasonable man will be overstated, as will the independence of the reasonable man from situational pressures.

Other effects

Many cognitive shortcomings not mentioned above are likely to be relevant to judicial performance. For example the difficulties which people experience when dealing with conditional probabilities (Eddy, 1982, shows severe difficulties in this regard experienced by another highly regarded professional group, medical doctors). People also express too much confidence in their probability judgments (Oskamp, 1965) and grossly underestimate the probability of extreme outcomes (Alpert and Raiffa, 1982; Lichtenstein *et al.*, 1977). Good reviews of the relevant literature, including many examples from applied (albeit non-legal) settings, may be found in Nisbett and Ross (1980), Kahneman *et al.* (1982) and Fischhoff *et al.* (1981). There are circumstances where biases are likely to cancel out, others where they may be compounded. Their existence should be demonstrated directly, and this depends on judicial willingness to co-operate, which can by no means be taken for granted.

On being critical of judges

In a sense, the content of this chapter has been unfairly negative. Its general thrust has been the suggestion that there are demonstrable ways in which what is practised departs from the rational (or normative, as it is referred to in the psychological literature − a usage which strikes us as outstandingly perverse). It is fair to say that there has been some dissatisfaction with straightforward normative approaches to decision-making. This dissatisfaction is well expressed by Wallsten (1980):

> although one might use laboratory experiments to study specific cognitive limitations or processes, it would be a mistake to imagine that there exists a small number of laws of decision behaviour that can be uncovered in the laboratory and then applied in a straightforward way to real world decisions. Thus, laboratory and observational studies should proceed hand in hand.

It is difficult to disagree with such a view, but who should do what next? Clearly, a start can be made in the laboratory by seeing whether the cognitive limitations which manifest themselves with other kinds of problem content also show up when the content is specifically linked to sentencing, and the writers are becoming engaged in such an attempt.

A complementary approach would be for psychologists to step back a little and try to understand the decisional processes through which judges go, rather than to prescribe the processes through which they should go. An attempt to set out on such an enterprise has been made by Schum (1980), although his work is directed towards determination of guilt rather than sentence, and is therefore not covered here. Schum's work should be read in conjunction with that of Cohen (1977) and of Crombag *et al.* (1975). Nonetheless, research should not be restricted to those issues which judges regard as problematic. Just as it is said that a fish is the last to recognise the existence of water, so judges may be least able to recognise the major kinds of decisional difficulty to which they are all prone.

CHAPTER 3

Reasons for sentence

Discussion of the relationship between speech and thought takes us into some of the deepest and murkiest theoretical waters of psychology. We do not wish to plumb those depths. Nonetheless we need to establish limits to the credibility of reasons. Later in the chapter we will present evidence of the mismatch between the reasons people give and their 'real' reasons, where these are knowable. For the moment, we will simply touch on the more basic arguments.

Limits on usable language also circumscribe what is thinkable. These limits are most in evidence when comparing cultures. Bourdieu (1977) argues that the linguistic field exercises censorship on discourse and thereby on what is thinkable. The medium, it seems, constrains not only the message but the range of possible messages. Frasure-Smith *et al.* (197) argue that parents' choice of language of instruction (when they have a choice) is guided by considerations of subtle effects on culture-specific modes of thought implied by that. This is also the message of the earlier work of Roger Brown (1956). Blackman (1981) makes similar points for offenders, and Lewis and Habert (1983) for politicians. Lemon (1975) concluded from research he conducted in Tanzania that language use in one role did not necessarily transfer to language use in another. Concepts formulated in separate languages of formal instruction in a school may not automatically transfer to their use in another language outside the school environment.

In short, what we say, and the way we say it, is both a function of the role in which we find ourselves and a determinant of the ways we can think. Consideration of judicial reasoning expressed in court must bear these things in mind.

Giving reasons – the *status quo*

David Thomas, the distinguished analyst of sentencing decisions, has long taken the view that sentencers should be required routinely to give reasons for their decisions (Thomas, 1963). There is already a limited requirement to this effect. In England and Wales, magistrates are required by section 20 of the Powers of Criminal Courts Act 1973 to give reasons for the imposition of a first sentence of imprisonment on a person aged twenty-one or over. As Ashworth (1977) points out, 'alternative measures can be quickly dismissed by reference to the gravity of the offence'. It is commonly observed in courts that reasons are often expressed as a terse formula – 'nature and gravity of the offence' – rather than as an explanation of thought-out justification specific to individual cases (see Rubin, 1966, for a discussion of this in the American context).

Much the same process was evident in, or rather can be inferred from, published justifications for the infliction of corporal punishment in prisons. These were recorded in the Annual Reports of the Prison Commissioners in England and Wales for each case in which that punishment was inflicted. For example, in Appendix 5 of the Annual Report for 1955 eleven cases of corporal punishment were recorded, six justified by 'the very serious nature' of the offence and five by the assertion that the offence was 'entirely unprovoked'. The year is not atypical. One of the writers in discussion with members of the Parole Board has heard it seriously argued that the fact that the reasons for parole refusal would be bound to be bland and uninformative constituted an argument for not giving reasons at all. Of a piece with such a justification is Lord Widgery's argument about why, in contrast to the requirements which apply in magistrates' courts, judges in the Crown Court should not be obliged to give reasons for a first sentence of imprisonment. Lord Widgery took the view that, in nine cases out of ten in the Crown Court, the gravity of the offence was the obvious reason for sentence, and one could not in every case 'spell out the judge's reasons and precise motives' (Ashworth, 1977).

In short, then, in a number of contexts within the criminal justice system, reasons tend to become bland, brief and standard. Indeed, in a story that may well be apocryphal, it is said that some magistrates' courts have rubber-stamps bearing the legend 'nature and gravity of the offence'. The phenomenon is not restricted to criminal justice settings. It is also to be found in circumstances as disparate as the specification of cause of death on death certificates and the evaluation of trainee pilot performance (see Flanagan, 1954). Apparently, when a statement of reasons is *standard* and *uncriticised*, a statement of reasons becomes worthless. The stressed qualifications are important, since it may well be that under certain circumstances, for example when justifications are required for exceptional rather than routine decisions, the same strictures may well not apply. The requirement of giving such reasons is part of the sentencing guidelines movement. However, the issue to be joined is less whether there are circumstances in which giving reasons for sentence may be desirable, but rather the prior question of what reasons, when given, represent. Although the relevant research has not been carried out on judges, the story the research tells is consistent enough to inspire confidence that we can generalise the findings to issues of judicial sentencing. The conclusion is the same as that to be reached from the theoretical considerations set out at the beginning of this chapter. Briefly, the reasons people give for their actions are usually not to be trusted.

On self-justification

Social psychologists must until relatively recently have seemed like ghouls to the casual reader of their academic journals. Would that all the experiments using electric shock were as neat and as well directed as that of Nisbett and Schachter (1966). People were simply asked to endure a series of shocks of increasing intensity, up to the point at which they found the pain intolerable. The experiment was then ended. The amperage of the last shock tolerated was what was measured. The neat trick lay in giving half the people who underwent the process a placebo pill, which contained nothing to produce any physical symptoms. Those taking the pill were, however, told that it would produce heart palpitations, breathing irregularities, hand tremor and butterflies in the stomach. These are the physical symptoms most people report when they have experienced electric shock. Thus people given shocks after taking the placebo pill would be able to attribute their symptoms to the pill rather than to the shock, and should in theory be able to tolerate more intense shocks before the point was reached at which the feelings produced by the shock were so intense that they could no longer be attributed to the effects of the pill. This prediction was fulfilled. People given the pill tolerated four times the amperage of those not given it. Since the pill was the only difference between the groups, some explanation along the general lines of that set out above must be right. The extra shock tolerance must in some way be linked to the pill and its attributed effects.

The most interesting part of the experiment has yet to be described. Not only did the people who underwent the experiment deny that they were aware of the effects of the pill, but when told what the hypothesis was, including the postulated process of attribution of the effects of the shock to the operation of the pill, people typically replied that, although no doubt other people went through such a process, they themselves had not. Their introspection had obviously not given them access to a process which must have taken place.

An even more striking result was obtained, again by Richard Nisbett, this time working with another colleague (Storms and Nisbett, 1970). In an experiment which was analogous to the shock study described already, they gave insomniacs a placebo pill. They informed one group of insomniacs that the pill would induce relaxation (lowered heart rate, breathing rate and body temperature, and a reduction in alertness). They told another group, given the same pill, that it would induce arousal (rapid heart rate, breathing irregularities, bodily warmth and alertness), which are the correlates of insomnia. The prediction of Storms and Nisbett was that those people who had a pill which they could blame, that is to say a pill which reproduced their unpleasant symptoms (in this case the symptoms of insomnia), would thereby attribute fewer of the symptoms to their real cause. This means that they would go to sleep more quickly than they normally did, while those given a pill with the claim that it would give them the symptoms of sleepiness would take longer than normal to go to sleep, because they would feel that the pill gave them even less reason than usual for the symptoms which they nonetheless experienced ('If I feel this awake even after the pill ...'). The results of the experiment turned out precisely as predicted, and to a spectacular extent. The people given a placebo and told that it produced high arousal went to sleep quickest. Those given no pill went to sleep next quickest. Those given the placebo and told it produced relaxation went to sleep last. When the experiment was explained to the people who had taken part in it, not only did they not believe that they had gone through the attribution process described to them, they considered the whole idea pretty implausible. Yet it had to be something like right, given the way people went to sleep!

The pattern of findings emerging from the work of Nisbett and his colleagues clearly shows how limited is the extent to which people have access to their own mental processes. Nisbett and Wilson (1977) conclude thus:

The explanations that subjects offer for their behaviour ... are so removed from the processes that investigators presume to have occurred as to give grounds for considerable doubt that there is direct access to these processes. This doubt would remain, it should be noted, even if it were eventually to be shown that processes other than those posited by investigators were responsible for the results of these experiments. Whatever the inferential process, the experimental method makes it clear that something about the manipulated stimuli produces the differential results. Yet subjects do not refer to these critical stimuli in any way in their reports on their cognitive processes.

Evidence of this kind of separation between mental processes and the verbal reports which purport to describe them is not only available from psychological experimentation. The description of the creative process by those who create is largely uninformative (see, for example, the collection of such accounts made by Ghiselin, 1952).

The evidence shows that people do not have access to their mental processes in ways which make them capable of the accurate verbal report of those processes. The evidence does not show that verbal report is *necessarily* inaccurate or inconsistent. For example, verbal report of thirst is likely to be an extremely accurate indicator of actual thirst. Sensation can thus be accessed in speech. 'I am thirsty' can be relied upon as self-report. Verbal consistency, however, is no guarantor of accuracy. The people subjected to the Nisbett experiments were quite consistent in their view that the pill which they had taken was irrelevant to their shock tolerance and to their insomnia. They were consistent, albeit wrong, in taking that view. How do reasons come to be consistent? One of the possible explanations is that we infer our reasons from our behaviour (see Bem, 1967; Bem and MaConnell, 1970). This is a 'radical behaviourist' approach to the topic. On this rather undignified view, the reason why people report themselves as liking wholemeal bread is because they find themselves selecting it from plates containing a variety of types of bread. The reason why a judge believes an offence is serious is because he finds himself (and others) passing long prison sentences on people convicted of such an offence. Put like that, of course, the idea sounds ludicrous. However, it alerts one to the role of self-perception at the behavioural levels as a basis for inferences as to reasons. This is not a hare which should be chased here because one does not have to follow Bem in order to remain sceptical of the judicial expression of reasons for sentence. We are conscious of the status of psychologists in the eyes of those who practise the law (stemming from lawyers' experience of seeing themselves avoiding psychologists, if the radical behaviourist view is right!). Those who judge truth by the pricking of their thumbs must be indulged as far as possible. The notion that we sit impotently inside our skulls looking out at what we do in order to guess what we think is an extreme one. But then so, as we hope to have shown, is the notion that we have complete access to our mental processes.

To restate briefly the argument of the last paragraphs, it is that verbal expressions of reasons for behaving in a particular way, whether that behaviour is judicial sentencing or any other complex behaviour, cannot confidently be accepted as accurate. This is evident both from psychological study and from honest introspection. It is true whether reasons seem bizarre or bland. For instance, we would not now regard confessions of witchcraft as credible accounts by people of their own actions, even in those cultural settings where witchcraft is still a socially favoured explanation. Similarly, it seems to us that offenders' accounts of crime on television and radio owe much to fashionable theories of crime. To be consistent, one should be as sceptical of such reasons as much as of judges' reasons for sentence. Such reasons are *post hoc* justifications of what was actually done rather than accurate representations of why it was done. We dealt in the last chapter with the observation that people exhibit quite spurious confidence in the predictability of an outcome once they know what that outcome was, the so-called 'knew-it-all-along' effect. There is no basis for supposing that one's own verbal reasoning should be exempt from the knew-it-all-along effect. In short, all one needs, to be sceptical of judicial reasons for sentence, is the suspicion that the sentence is an element in its own justification, that, for example, the passing of a sentence of imprisonment is a factor in the enunciation of reasons for passing a prison sentence. This proposition is absolutely untestable. A proper test would require an expression of sentencing purpose a microsecond before a decision as to sentence was reached. If reasons given then were to correspond to those given for the sentence when it was reached, the position taken here is wrong. It is relevant to note, though, that in the legal problems whose solution was studied by Crombag *et al.* (1975) a provisional decision was taken early in the process, and the relationship between current situation and outcome filled in later. If sentencing decisions are taken like this, it strengthens our scepticism about reasons.

Reasons for reasons

In her detailed research on the process of mitigation, Shapland (1981) rehearses the reasons for giving reasons. She concludes, 'although there is considerable feeling that some form of reasons should be given, there is doubt about what these reasons represent'. Jackson (1971) writes:

The explanations or reasons given by the judges have become more various ... an offender whose sentence has in fact been determined by the current rating of ... an offence may be given a reason for such a sentence in terms of one or more items of the present judicial repertoire. It is most difficult to know whether these 'reasons' for sentences have any effect on the offender or on potential offenders or whether they are just so much good sounding talk to be expected of those who are set in authority over us.

Gottfredson *et al.* (1978) produce a rather different argument against reasons:

Let us consider provision of the following reason in the case of an armed bank robber sentenced to a prison term, 'You have committed an armed robbery in which lives were potentially endangered. You are not a suitable candidate for probation because of the seriousness of your offence, combined with your prior record of two convictions during the past year. In addition, you were on probation at the time of the present offence and have a history of severe heroin usage.' Many would agree that this is a substantial narrative reason for Judge Lenient's imposition of a two-year prison term. However when one agrees that it appears to be an equally good reason for Judge Moderate's imposition of a five-year prison term or Judge Severe's imposition of a ten-year prison term, it should be readily apparent that even the articulation of the criteria used without the weights given to them is not likely to produce the desired effect.

How to believe your reasons

Once giving reasons for behaviour is recognised as more than a straightforward report, it is perhaps worth trying to address the issue of why people feel as though they have direct access to their own mental process. Nisbett and Wilson (1977) (see also Ericsson and Simon, 1980) have tentatively identified four circumstances in which confidence in direct access is particularly high. They argue that confidence in one's reasons will be high when:

(1) Only a few reasons are possible.
(2) The events preceding the decision are clear in memory or image.
(3) The reasoning is culturally plausible.
(4) The same reasons have been given in justification of the same decision previously.

Let us take the four circumstances individually and see how they relate to the process of giving reasons for sentence. It is entirely plausible that when the choice of reason lies between a few alternatives (e.g. nature of offence, length of record, breach of trust) it is likely to be trusted more than if it lies between many. If a judge has clear recollection of the facts of a case they may appear more clearly as justifications of sentence. If the reasons are well tried they will invite more confidence in their truth. The fourth circumstance associated with confidence is particularly interesting, because a quite well-known piece of research about reasoning in the courtroom bears on the point. The relevance of the research is only indirect, because it deals with sentencers' acceptance or rejection of other people's proffered reasons rather than with the formulation of sentencers' own reasons. The research in question was carried out by Taylor (1972). He obtained, from a number of magistrates, views about the credibility of various possible accounts given by offenders of the reasons for their actions. These reasons included: having a mental blackout before the crime; being overcome by an irresistible urge; coming from a neighbourhood where the behaviour was the rule rather than the exception; cold deliberate choice, and so on. In this way, and in the absence of any other evidence which could be brought to bear on the reasoning, Taylor showed that what he called motivational accounts, reasons, were believed by magistrates when they were culturally plausible. For instance, motivational accounts of rape invoking irresistible urge are culturally plausible, and were believed, whereas invoking the justification that one comes from an area where rape is general, is not. In contrast, cheque fraud justified by irresistible urge is implausible. Offenders who had read the Nisbett research referred to earlier might prefer to answer the question 'Why did you do it?' with 'I don't have access to that information. I could give you an account of which I would be confident and which you are likely to believe, but that doesn't make it true.' Such an answer could not be guaranteed a sentencing discount for honesty!

Before leaving the topic of the Taylor research, perhaps it is permissible to expand a little on the common bases of the four criteria for maximum credibility of expressed reasons. Taylor was concerned with the notion of motivational accounts. If the literature is to be believed (see Nisbett and Ross, 1980) it seems likely that the availability and representativeness heuristics underlie the four criteria. Heuristics are strategies of judgment, and, applied to the giving of reasons, the two strategies could be characterised as follows: the availability heuristic operates by the selection of that motivational account which is most accessible in the processes of perception, memory or construction from imagination. The representativeness heuristic would suggest that people operate by assessing the extent to which a motive is deemed representative of motives characteristic of the category of behaviour under consideration. In other words, people will attribute motives and believe the attribution of motives on the basis of how available the motive is to them and how typical it is seen to be of motives applied to the class of events under consideration. To take an example from the Taylor research, irresistible impulse is a commonly expressed account, as is temporary irresponsibility (mistake, blackout, etc.). These are therefore highly available motivational accounts. They are featured in the repertoire of justifications of most people. Taking a particular class of events, for example rape, certain kinds of motivational account are typically brought to bear on such behaviour. Irresistible impulse is a good example. Irresistible impulse is thus a highly representative motivational account for application to rape events. *Mutatis mutandis*, one could apply the heuristics to judicial reasoning. The repertoire of reasons for sentence includes nature and gravity of offence, prior record of offencer, offender's age, and so on. These are *available*. Sexual offences against children would evoke 'public protection' as the most *representative* of the repertoire of accounts available.

There is good evidence that availability and representativeness heuristics do guide human thinking, and some of the implications of this will be outlined later in this book (in Chapter 5). These heuristics are generally reliable bases for action, but can obviously lead astray those whom they help. To take an extremely simple example for the availability heuristic. Suppose you sample a word at random from an English text. Is it more likely that the word starts with a K or that K is its third letter? People answer such a question by comparing the availability of the two categories, i.e. by assessing the ease with which instances of the two categories come to mind. It is much easier to think of words that start with a K than of words where K is the third letter. If the judgment asked for is informed by the heuristic of availability, then people will assert that words that start with K are the more frequent. People do this, and they are wrong. A typical text contains twice as many words with K as third letter (Tversky and Kahneman, 1973).

There is much evidence to suggest that biases stemming from both representativeness and availability heuristics operate in social judgment generally and, although we know of no direct evidence from the study of motives (except from the Taylor study), there is no obvious reason to suppose that it would prove an exception. What kinds of accounts are likely to be favoured in credibility by the two heuristics? Unlike other social judgments, assertions of the reasons why we act as we do are essentially untestable. It is difficult to think of any examples of clear relationships between reasons and behaviour (excluding those based on direct sensations like thirst). While estimates of the number of people unemployed in your area could be changed by scrutiny of statistics, visits to Job Centres, and so on, judgments about motives could not. What kinds of motivational account are liable to be favoured as credible by the two heuristics? Taking accounts of crime as the starting-point, the obviously available accounts would be those given commonly as excuses for crime. Our common-sense theories of crime, implicating poverty, unemployment, youth and alcohol, provide explanations which will be more representative, i.e. occur in more of the cases, and be more available, because they are given voice more often, than other explanations. In the same way as the Nisbett research gives us evidence that we cannot summon accurate accounts for behaving as we do, the availability and representativeness heuristics provide us with mechanisms whereby we come to use and accept a particular vocabulary of motives, irrespective of their relationship to the behaviour they are designed to account for. The motives take on an existence of their own. The more they are used the more they are believed (by both heuristics) and therefore the more they are used, and so on, in a process whose culmination teeters on the edge of clichéd excuses. That is a state of affairs familiar to the sentencer in the terse and uninformative reasons for sentence described earlier, and also for the sentencer in the maintenance of his commonsense beliefs and its causes based upon the justifications offered to him by the offender, the social inquiry report, the defence counsel and the media. This is not, of course, to say that the reasons offered are *necessarily* wrong. For there ever to be new excuses, one needs to have situations in which evidence in individual cases points almost overwhelmingly to a particular causal explanation that it is accepted, and starts on the royal road to increased use. The ascent of the pre-menstrual syndrome as an excuse for some crimes by women is perhaps an example of this process.

The thrust of this chapter has been to suggest that a proper understanding of principles of sentencing should not be based on judicially expressed reasons for passing particular sentences, or on judges' general pronouncements about sentencing policy. An understanding of sentencing practice and policy must be based on empirical examination of the variables with which sentence choice co-varies, and how it co-varies. For example, although unemployment is, as we will argue in a later chapter, a major source of criminal justice excuses, it is reliably associated with more, not with less, severe sentencing (see Crow, 1980; Jardine *et al.*, 1983). So in the case of employment, at least, sentencing practice and an excuse for crime co-vary in the way opposite to that which one might expect.

Disparaging the reliability of reasons given as indicators of real reasons should set up in the reader an attitude of scepticism about reasons, not one of rejection of reasons as worthless in the court context. If reasons have a place in court, it is because they are defensible, not because they are true. When available for challenge, reasons invite people in the court to behave as if they were true, to test, challenge and appeal against. Even spurious reasons (and, it is contended, no reason is known not to be spurious) may, when challenged, enforce patterns of sentencing which correspond with what the practice would be if the reason were the real one. In fact, in informing court practice, it may become the real one. It is this relationship between justifications for unusual decisions and the modification of underlying policy which is one of the more exciting aspects of the sentencing guideline movement (discussed in Chapter 1). But, it is important to note, the attack on reasoning is necessary for the provision of reasons to be a starting-point for something more than a hollow and inadvertent parody of open justice.

So far, we have discussed reasons for sentence within a fairly narrow compass. Reasons for sentence are sometimes expressed in grander terms, like deterrence and retribution. To complement the discussion so far, and to justify further our scepticism about the value of expressions of sentencing purpose to explain the origins of sentencing practice, in the next chapter we will go through the conventional repertoire of sentencing purposes, guess what sentencing practice would look like if these principles were adhered to, and finally consider some data on what in fact predicts sentencing decisions.

CHAPTER 4

The purposes of sentencing

In Chapter 2 we described the relationships between behaviour and the reasons given for behaviour. We tried to give examples of the relevance of that discussion to the sentencing act. Yet in one sense the discussion has taken place in a vacuum. No general typology of sentencing purposes has yet been attempted. We have expressed scepticism of the bland, standard reasons given in justifying the first prison sentence, and we have supplied evidence that reasons given are not to be trusted. However, we have not given sentencing analysts a fair run. A typology of sentencing purposes could emerge at a number of different levels. It could consist of a listing and classification of reasons which sentencers state to be relevant. A reading of the last chapter will suggest why we regard such an approach to be misguided. An alternative way, which stands a better chance of prescribing a coherent sentencing policy, consists of a specification of those purposes which sentencing might be intended to achieve, and an elaboration of the kinds of sentencing patterns which could be based on each sentencing purpose, deciding whether these patterns are distinguishable and if so how, and then deciding how these patterns correspond to the normal run of sentencing practice, trying to avoid at all stages the use of the word 'theory' as one which, Walker (1980) warns, 'makes Anglo-American judges pull back their safety catches'.

At the most general level, two types of punishment justification may be distinguished, retributive and utilitarian. As to retributive theories, 'vindication in the sense of society's claim to amends for the harm done, or for outraged feelings, fairness to the law-abiding and proportionality of punishment to the seriousness of the offence may respectively be treated as the bases of retributive theories' (Cross, 1981). Utilitarian theories have as their underlying assumption the view that human suffering must be minimised, both that of the potential victims of crime and that of criminals. This implies prevention of crime by the method which is minimally intrusive on the life of the offender but which is effective.

The two most readily distinguishable strands in the retributive tradition are retribution proper and denunciation. Other distinctions (see Walker, 1980) may also be made within this tradition. Retribution is the notion that the punishment should be what an offender in some sense deserves. It is characterised by its concentration on the past, on the offence rather than on what the offender might or might not do in the future. Denunciation is the sentencing purpose which suggests that the function of the sentence is simply to express society's abhorrence of the offending behaviour being denounced.

As for utilitarian theories, the major specific sentencing purposes which they contain are deterrence, incapacitation and rehabilitation. The principle of deterrence is itself properly divided into special and general deterrence. Appeal to the sentencing purpose of special deterrence implies direction of the sentence at the person sentenced. It characterises the offender as a rational optimiser of the consequences of his actions. Its success depends upon the transformation of an anticipated net gain resulting from the commission of an offence into an anticipated net loss, by an increase in the anticipated debit side of the equation. That is to say, it increases the disincentives to committing an offence again. Appeal to the principle of general deterrence implies the direction of the sentence at everyone except the person sentenced. It characterises the citizen as a rational optimiser of the consequences of his actions. Its success depends upon the transformation of an anticipated net gain obtained by the commission of an offence by an increase in the anticipated net loss. General and special deterrence differ in that the former operates through remembering the lash on another's back, and the latter through remembering it on one's own.

The sentencing purpose of incapacitation is fulfilled in so far as someone is prevented from committing crime. The death penalty is the obvious example of complete incapacitation. Disqualification from driving is an example of partial incapacitation.

The last of the major utilitarian sentencing purposes is rehabilitation. This is intended to operate through changing the person in such a way as to make him less inclined to commit crime. In contrast to deterrence, where the aim of crime reduction is to be achieved by increasing disincentives, rehabilitation is intended to achieve the same end by changing the offender's inclinations in other ways.

These brief descriptions of sentencing purpose can be no more than caricatures of the sophisticated accounts to be found elsewhere (see, for example, Walker, 1980; Cross, 1981). In particular, relationships between the purposes are very complex. Cross (1981) sees denunciation as a kind of long-term deterrence. 'The fact that people are punished for crime is believed to build up an abhorrence of it over the years and thus, to reduce the number of those who would even remotely contemplate it.' Making the point more colourfully, Walker (1980) asserts: 'The denouncer is either a crypto-reducer or a quasi-punisher.'

Our immediate purpose in making the conventional distinctions between theories of punishment is to see how clearly distinguishable they might be in sentencing practice. Let us first assume that, the more serious a crime is, the more we disapprove of it and the more we would like to reduce its incidence. How would a judge operating according to each of the sentencing purposes set out above relate offence seriousness to sentence severity? When incapacitation is the informing principle, the more serious the offence the longer the time for which the offender would properly be incapacitated, thereby preventing more of the serious crime. When deterrence is the informing principle, the more serious the offence the more severe the sentence, on the ground that the more serious the offence, the more the offender and other citizens should be provided with disincentives against committing it. When rehabilitation is the sentencing purpose, the more serious the offence, the more damaged must be the personality of the offender, and hence the longer he must be detained by the state in order to repair the damage. For both retribution and denunciation, *ipso facto* more serious offences merit more punishment.

Put like that, the awful truth emerges that all sentencing purposes lead to the prediction of the same relationship between offence seriousness and sentence severity. One could go through the same process with other variables, like criminal record. The worse the criminal record the more incapacitation and deterrence are prudent, the more rehabilitation is needed and the more retribution and denunciation are justified. In fact, it is remarkably difficult to generate ideal types of sentencing practice based either on single principles or on combinations of sentencing principles which differ from each other. It should be easier when one considers a wider range of possible sentences and it should be particularly easy when the sentence is marked with its purpose – for example Borstal Training has clearly been a penal alternative with a rehabilitative purpose – or has it? Under section 3(1) of the Criminal Justice Act 1961, a sentence of imprisonment shall not be passed on a person of an age for Borstal Training, unless it is for not more than six months and not less than three years. Thus a sentence of 'training' is regarded as an all-purpose middle-severity sentence as well.

If one attempts to describe how, say, a retributive judge would behave in ways that would distinguish him from a rehabilitator, from the perspective of an observer who had access only to the pattern of sentencing, then the predicted difference would almost certainly reduce itself to a discussion of the rate at which punishment increased as other relevant variables increased. For example, one might predict that an emphasis on deterrence may lead to more severe sentences for trivial offences than would be consequent on an emphasis on retribution. An emphasis on deterrence may lead to a closer relationship between offence prevalence and sentence severity. One might predict that more rehabilitation-minded judges give more probation and community service orders than other judges, although even here the prediction is contestible.

The difference in judicial philosophy which ought to be most transparent from judicial practice is that between deterrent and retributive sentencing. After all, do we not refer to particularly severe sentences as deterrent or exemplary (presumably on the basis that general deterrent sentencing is sentencing which makes an example of the offender)? Are not deterrent sentences therefore readily distinguishable from retributive sentence? They are if one believes judicial reasons. If you don't believe judicial reasons, and we have already given grounds for scepticism, deterrent or exemplary sentencing may simply be the *post hoc* justification of more severe sentencing on the basis of whatever happen to be the normal (available and representative) grounds for more severe sentencing. This possibility is quite consistent with the utterances of judges. For example, in the case of *Campbell* ((1979) 1 CR.App.Rep. (S)), the distinguished judges hearing the appeal pronounced as follows: 'We have come to the conclusion that as far as this case is concerned, the prevalence of this sort of offence requires us to impose upon you a deterrent sentence ... I have referred to what [you] had done. It was the right sentence *for this offence*' (emphasis added).

Similarly nice distinctions between processes justifying the same end by different means are evident elsewhere. Fallon (1975) distinguishes deterrent and exemplary sentences. Deterrent sentences are justified by 'the prevalence of a particular crime in an area or the sudden increase in the type of crime in an area'. They operate through the neglect by the court of features which would otherwise be factors in mitigation, like youth or the absence of a prior record. Exemplary sentences, on the other hand, are those 'in excess of the level for the offence'. 'The Court of Appeal tends to view exemplary sentences as opposed to deterrent sentences with disfavour', according to Fallon.

Research has been conducted on the relationship between a judge's verbal expression of his sentencing philosophy and his sentencing practice. Wheeler *et al.* (1968) and McFatter (1978) both, as a result of such a comparison, produced fairly complex representations of the relationship. Since relationships found in the two studies were largely inconsistent with each other, it seems reasonable to conclude that the confusion in principle about what would in practice distinguish judges with different philosophies is mirrored by inconclusiveness in the research directly addressing the issue. In the case of this research, though, it would be less than honest of us if we failed to admit that we find ourselves in a no-lose position. If the Wheeler and McFatter research had shown a consistent relationship between philosophy and practice, we could glibly have dismissed the work by saying that judges chose a sentencing philosophy as an inference from their sentencing practice on the basis of conventional reasoning. For example, deterrent purposes may be an inference from harsh sentencing for relatively trivial offences, and rehabilitative purposes from relatively lenient sentencing in a particular case. We blush to place ourselves in a position where we can justify ourselves whatever the outcome of the research. However, if we are right in our view of sentencing, this is precisely the skill at which judges are adept.

The basic point of the last chapter was that people do not have such privileged access to their thought processes as to enable us to infer that the justifications which they give for their behaviour are accurate. The basic proposition of this chapter up to this point is that it is virtually impossible to infer sentencing purpose from sentencing practice. Alternative courses of action within a very wide range are compatible with a very wide range of justifications. Put the two together and the possibility exists for the development of a rhetoric of sentencing, which is believed by those who express it, which is self-perpetuating and which is of not the slightest use in understanding the sentencing process. By this sort of reasoning, the behaviourally oriented psychologist would come to see the legal literature on sentencing as epiphenomenal. For him, the question would not be how particular sentences are justified, but how choice of sentence co-varies with information available to the judge. It is to this issue that we now turn.

What predicts sentence?

The most important research in this area has been that of Leslie Wilkins and his colleagues. Because the work began with studies of parole in the United States, its relevance to sentencing and parole in the United Kingdom must be established.

In the United Kingdom, courts determine within limits how long someone stays in prison. Prison and parole authorities are also important in determining length of incarceration by withholding remission and/or parole, but for present purposes all that needs to be said is that courts are relevant in determining sentence length. Courts are much less relevant in determining sentence length in the *traditional* North American jurisdiction, where the sentencing decision is indeterminate, being of the form 'one to ten years', for example. In such a situation the effective time-fixing agent is the paroling authority, not the court. The Wilkins research on parole, then, has important parallels with court sentencing, and in fact Wilkins and his colleagues moved easily from the parole board to the court while maintaining their overall strategy of research.

The first stage of this strategy involved modelling the penal decision. That is, equations were set up to predict likely sentence or parole outcomes. As Wilkins (1980) writes, 'the feelings of scientists are not the criterion by which the scientific method is assessed! If it is possible to predict situations, events or behaviours by the use of formulas, the scientist then has a form of "understanding" or "explanation".' The means by which such an understanding was reached in the Wilkins strategy was by the examination of a large body of data to find the single piece of information which, on its own, is the most useful in predicting a particular outcome, for instance release on parole after a particular length of custody.

The next stage was to examine all the other data for the item of information which adds most to the predictive power of the first, and then to examine all the remaining data to choose that item which adds most to the predictive power of the first two. A point is soon reached at which extra information adds only trivially to the predictive power. At this stage, an understanding of the decision being modelled can be said to have been reached. It was a statistical approach of this kind which underlay the Wilkins research. As may readily be imagined, the description given here in no way reflects the fullness of the approach, which was both technically and substantively innovative. Nonetheless, hopefully it captures the spirit of the work.

It is of crucial importance to recall the context of the parole decision-making project. It involved an embattled US Federal Parole Board which was being criticised for its apparently idiosyncratic decision-making but was unable to defend itself against such criticism by making reference to any explicit Board policy. The purpose was, in consequence, 'to provide a feedback device for ... members ... of the United States Board of Parole concerning the relationships between their evaluation of specific case factors ... and paroling decisions. From these relationships, based upon a sample of case decisions, implicit paroling policies may be inferred and made explicit' (Hoffman, 1972).

What is policy? It is action directed towards the realisation of a purpose or set of purposes. How shall policy be known? It shall be known by the recognition of patterns in decisions which are consistent with the expressed purpose. It is of interest, in the light of our earlier discussions of the ineffability of reasons, even to the decision-maker himself, that the Wilkins research represents an example of the process of inferring policy from observed patterns of decisions, rather than the patterning of decisions on the basis of policy. It is just such a counter-intuitive process that, we argued above, may lead judges to make *post hoc* inferences of their sentencing purposes. The US Federal Parole Board obviously thought to establish their policy by engaging Wilkins and his colleagues to analyse what they had been doing!

The Wilkins research revealed that two variables, severity of initial offence and prediction of parole outcome, by themselves indicate time spent in prison after the initial parole hearing. Prediction of parole outcome is itself a function of a prisoner's disciplinary record while in prison (Hoffman, 1972). The high level of prediction accuracy was achieved despite the relative crudity of the variables used. To summarise, then, release on licence in the federal parole system is predictable from the seriousness of the original offence and the prison disciplinary record. Hoffman (1972) writes of the matrix of values formed by these two variables that it may be used 'to make explicit presently implicit paroling policies. For example, it would appear that a difference of one level of severity (seriousness) shifts the decision ± three months.' This type of matrix came to be used as a baseline for individual case decisions, being the kernel of the guidelines approach described earlier in the book. For the moment, though, our purpose is simply to demonstrate that penal decision-makers, both on the parole board and in the judiciary, are able to operate, in fact do operate, largely on the basis of a few pieces of basic information. Good fittings of prediction equations to real-life decisions can be achieved by the use of a very small number of items of information.

After the success of their parole research, Leslie Wilkins, Don Gottfredson and their colleagues approached judges in the federal courts. Funding difficulties led to the shifting of the initiative from the federal system to state courts. In the event, two primary juris-dictions were the subject of study, or rather were partners in the research, as Wilkins would prefer. The jurisdictions were the County of Denver, Colorado, and the State of Vermont.

The researchers first collected all factors that authorities in the literature or the judiciary on our Steering and Police Committee considered relevant to reaching the sentencing decision. Some 205 items of information from 200 randomly selected sentencing decisions in each of the two participating courts were collected. We also tried to gather all the information which was available to the judge for consideration in deciding about an actual sentence. (Kress *et al.*, 1976)

Armed with this information, the research team went through essen-tially the same process as was described earlier in relation to parole, namely to find those characteristics of offence and offender which accounted for the largest percentage of variation in the sentencing decision. The variables which emerged as central were essentially the same as those which had emerged from the earlier work on parole, with the unsurprising exception that the record of bad behaviour which was relevant to the decision was the offender's criminal record rather than the disciplinary record in prison. 'Our analyses indicated that the two most influential groupings of information items were those measuring the seriousness of the current offence and the extent of the offender's criminal record' (Kress *et al.*, 1976). Seventy-five to eighty per cent of the variance in sentencing decisions was accounted for by these two factors taken together (Wilkins, 1983, personal communication). Once again, the primary determinants of penal decision-making are found to be comparatively simple, consisting essentially of judgments of seriousness of offence committed and previous criminal behaviour.

Is there any evidence from this side of the Atlantic that these are the crucial determinants of sentencing and paroling decisions? There is some such evidence, both meagre experimental evidence and rather more substantial statistical evidence, although in much of what follows there is a danger of descending into the self-evident. The point at issue is how important the factors of offence seriousness and criminal record are, whether they are simply two important factors among many, or alternatively are absolutely pre-eminent as determinants of penal decisions.

There is much less scope for time-setting in the English parole scene than in the United States, because of the former's tradition of determinate sentencing. Notwithstanding this, it is fascinating that the English research on parole selection produces such similar results. Because of its importance, and because we have found the work to be little known and its significance little understood, we will describe it in some detail. The study is one of a series of empirical studies of parole in England and Wales published as Nuttall *et al.* (1977). It concerned an analysis of the decisions of local review committees (LRCs). An LRC exists for every prison holding parole-eligible prisoners. It constitutes the first, prison-based tier of parole decision-making. LRCs are 'probably the most important part of the selection structure; for the majority of cases that they find unsuitable for parole their decision is effectively final, and since May 1973 ... this has been so also for a growing majority of cases recommended as suitable' (Nuttall *et al.*, 1977). The aim of the research was to determine the factors used by LRCs in making the decision to recommend release on licence. In principle, the method used to do this was similar to that described in connection with the Wilkins research. In the English research the technique was a statistical method known as the Automatic Interaction Detector (whose acronym is shared with a better-known technique of no particular relevance to the judiciary). The technique 'isolates the variables most strongly related to recommendation rates ... At each stage a group is sub-divided into two using the split of the particular variable which explains most variance.' In the parole research described, twenty-two variables gleaned from information in parole dossiers were linked to LRC decisions on 878 men undergoing their first parole review during the first five months of 1972, and on 804 men being considered at their second or subsequent review during the same period. The information included age, prison offences, time in last job, and a host of other criminal and social variables.

At first review, previous convictions, living arrangements on release (for those with three or more previous convictions), sentence length and the experience of two or more periods of custody as a juvenile (for those with less satisfactory living arrangements and short sentences) were the factors most strongly associated with the decision to recommend release. Thus, in all but one split, the relevant factors were all to do with criminal history or sentence length. If, when we get to a discussion of sentence length, we can show that sentence length is determined by offence seriousness, the parole release recommendation may be seen, as in the American case, to be largely a function of offence seriousness and criminal record. When the AID analysis was performed on prisoners facing their second or subsequent review, sentence length and criminal record continued to be decisive of the outcome, although the emphasis on offences against prison discipline increased in importance as the most relevant type of 'criminal history'. Also as might have been anticipated given the proximity in time of second and subsequent reviews to the expected date of release, living arrangements on release came to have more influence on release recommendations.

A curious sidelight on the parole research is afforded by the finding that in 86 per cent of LRC decisions, the decision appeared to follow the recommendation as to release made by the prison's assistant governor. It thus looks very much as though LRCs comply with the recommendation of a member of the prison's senior staff even though the basis on which that recommendation is made is not one about which the assistant governor has any special experience or insight. It is, alas, impossible to decide whether this picture is produced by the exercise of real influence by the assistant governor over LRC decisions or is simply a coincidence of decision rules. In either event, the decisions made are largely based on information similar to that found to inform the US Federal Board of Parole.

The practice which has developed following the enactment of section 35 of the 1972 Criminal Justice Act seems to confirm the centrality of offence seriousness in parole decision-making. Certain categories of offender may, under that provision, be released without reference to the Parole Board if the LRC recommends parole unanimously. To date, two categories of prisoner have been identified: where (1) the sentence is not longer than two years; or (2) the sentence is not longer than four years and the crime does not involve violence, sex, arson or drug trafficking. Thus the two factors chosen to structure the mechanics of parole release may both be regarded as measures of offence seriousness, one direct (offence type) and one indirect (sentence length). Those committing graver offences as thus measured are excluded from the fast lane to freedom offered by section 35.

Parole has been treated before sentencing itself in this part of the book. This has the advantage of reflecting the order in which the relevant American work was conducted and came to be applied. It has the disadvantage of requiring the reader to take on trust the assertion that sentence length and offence seriousness co-vary strongly.

Historically it is otiose to seek to demonstrate the centrality of offence seriousness to sentence severity, at least in the non-trivial part of the range of sentencing alternatives. The relationship was so much taken for granted that the earliest empirical studies of offence seriousness (Messedaglia, 1866; Mayr, 1917) took their measures of offence seriousness from statistics of sentencing practice. The whole notion of tariff sentencing is based upon the idea. Although legal restraints on sentencing are limited, there is a clear awareness among judges about the range of sentences which are 'right' for different kinds of offence. Departures from this on the high side may attract reversal of the sentencing decision upon appeal. Readers willing to accept the rough equivalence of the dimensions of offence seriousness and sentence severity should at this point skip to the beginning of the last paragraph of this chapter. A convenient basis for examination of the relationship between judgments of offence seriousness and sentence length is to be found in the proposals of the Advisory Council on the Penal System in its 1978 report on maximum sentences of imprisonment. The Council's central proposal was to establish new maximum sentences by reference to the sentence length below which 90 per cent of all sentences of immediate imprisonment fell. This 90 per cent standard provides a rough and ready measure of the sentence length appropriate to very bad instances of particular offences. Because, as we will describe later, there is a high degree of consensus between groups of people as to the relative seriousness of offences, this is a context in which the judgments of most readers will not deviate wildly from the judgments of people generally. For those readers who wish to consult the Report, the most cursory examination of Table 2 of Appendix A will reveal that those offences for which a high 90 per cent standard is specified are also those which one would judge to be serious (apart from the more delightfully incomprehensible offences, like 'misconduct of master or member of crew' and 'assisting offenders', a description of unrivalled and stunning opacity). For those readers not ready to consult the Report, the following list is taken from the table on p. 81 of the Report by taking the first offence specified for each of the 90 per cent standard levels (excluding two more complex offence descriptions). The reader is invited to rank these offences in order of seriousness.

Possession of drugs
Possession of drugs with intent to supply
Indecent assault on a man
Robbery
Rape
Murder

It is likely that the reader will have rated offences near the bottom of the list as more serious, and indeed the 90 per cent standards gets longer as one reads upwards in the list.

Another demonstration of correspondence between intuitive judgments of seriousness and notional sentence length may be discerned in the Alverstone Memorandum of 1901 on 'normal punishments in certain kinds of crimes' despite various archaisms of offence description. The Memorandum is reproduced both in the Advisory Council Report cited above and in Jackson (1971).

One of us (Fitzmaurice, 1981), in a series of experiments more fully described in Chapter 6, set out to explore the concept of proportionality in judicial sentencing. One of those studies involved asking two Crown Court judges to sentence a series of 'paper' cases. Fitzmaurice then calculated the percentage of the variance in sentence length attributable to differences in the judged seriousness of the offence. In the case of these two judges, 77 per cent and 98 per cent of the variation in sentence length was accounted for by variation in judgments of offence seriousness. Fitzmaurice comments thus on the contrast between the complexity of the judges' self-reports and the simplicity of the actual relationship between offence gravity and sentence.

One would nearly forget that most of the variance in sentence length was explained by the variable 'seriousness of offence'. In fact, the picture which emerged here is one in which the judge claims to take into consideration factors related to the offender even though he emphasises the illogicality of the approach. The idea projected is that of a person who weighs all factors and makes adjustments once everything has gone through the mental mixer, to take the future and past of the offender, the offence, the victim and society into account. The story told by the R^2 (statistic expressing extent of explanation of variation in sentence length by the offence's seriousness) is different.

The view of offence seriousness as pre-eminent in determining, along with criminal record, the severity of sentence passed, while consistent with judicial practice, is at odds with judicial reservations about the notion of a tariff. This according to Cross (1981) is 'anathema to some judges' because gravity of offence is only one of the reasons for the choice of a sentence, because gravity is a complex concept, and

the statement that no two cases are alike is none the less true for being a truism; finally, any suggestion that the length of a prison sentence can be determined without reference to the conglomeration of circumstances which passes under the name of the 'human factor' would be unacceptable to a large, though by no means all-inclusive, number of people concerned with sentencing practice.

Nonetheless, it seems clear that the two variables identified are indeed central to sentencing, whatever the complexities, real and imagined, of the principle of taking each case on its merits. Yet the notion of offence seriousness seems unpromisingly vague to some as an underpinning of our subsequent analysis. Before using the concept further, we must establish whether it is robust enough for our purposes. Chapter 5 addresses this issue.

Offence gravity

The word 'gravity' is the lawyer's equivalent of the social scientist's preferred 'seriousness'. The lawyer's usage is interesting because of its overtones of weight and importance. Rossi *et al.* (1974) argue that 'the seriousness of criminal acts represents a conceptual dimension of criminality indispensable in everyday discourse, in legal theory and practice, and in sociological work'. If justice as fairness requires the visitation of offences of varying gravity with penal consequences of varying severity, an understanding of the nature of judgments of offence seriousness is essential. For such an important concept, offence seriousness seems disturbingly unspecific. Some writers have tried to substitute more precise variables. For example, Chambers (1967) and Bryant *et al.* (1968) used more specific terms derived from their particular purpose in developing a scale. Their concern was the optimisation of police deployment. They thus chose to substitute police officers' assessments of the value of preventing a crime or the value of detecting a crime, for the subjective assessment of its seriousness. From the similarity of the results obtained, it seems likely that, whatever the instructions given to the policemen, they ended up using the more general concept of offence seriousness anyway. A similar phenomenon has been observed with other groups (Pease *et al.* 1976). Bryant *et al.* observed:

In both the main and supplementary questionnaires it had been suggested to subjects that the values assigned to detection should be based on an estimate of the number of additional crimes likely to be committed if no detection were made. None of the subjects expressed any disagreement with the principle and we had therefore expected that detecting a crime with a low detection rate and a highly probability of being repeated if not detected, like a break-in offence, would attract a higher detection score, relative to its prevention score, than detecting a crime without these characteristics. The fact that the ratio of detection value to prevention value remains constant over ... crimes ...

simply suggests that the ratings awarded were based only on a consideration of the relative seriousness of the different crimes, and that no allowance was made for the differences in the preventive work of different types of detection.

Despite the tendency to revert to assessments of offence gravity when asked about more specific judgments, no self-respecting social scientist should evince any satisfaction with a concept as fuzzy as that of offence seriousness. Stephen Gottfredson, in an as yet unpublished monograph, draws an analogy between offence seriousness and the 'bigness' of sticks, and Rossi *et al.* (1974) draw one between offence seriousness and prestige. In both analogies, we may feel we can recognise examples when we see them (a big stick, a prestigious job, a serious offence) while remaining unable to specify how their attributes combine to yield that impression. We may be sure that length, diameter and weight contribute something to the bigness of a stick, and injury, loss and damage to the seriousness of an offence, but even if these attributes turn out to be reliably associated statistically with judgments of bigness or seriousness, there remain not inconsiderable difficulties in comparing long narrow sticks with short thick sticks as to their bigness, and in comparing in terms of their relative seriousness the profitable robbery with little injury to the victim with the low-yielding robbery involving the infliction of much injury. It is not fanciful to see the particular problems sentencers encounter in dealing with attempts, and in particular with unintended consequences (see, e.g., Ashworth, 1975) as a reflection of the difficulty in producing a combinatorial rule for elements of judged offence seriousness.

However, we anticipate ourselves in embarking upon this discussion here. Before taking the trouble to search for its determinants, we must ask what is in some senses a more fundamental question, namely whether there is social consensus about judgments of offence seriousness. Rossi *et al.* confirm that 'to be of theoretical or practical use, a measure of crime "seriousness" requires that a society display consensus about the order of seriousness of specific criminal acts.' We have argued in this book up to this point that, while the rhetoric of sentencing involves a 'mental mixing' of a range of factors, the evidence from cognitive psychology suggests strongly that we should be sceptical of accepting the verbal representations of their reasoning by sentencers literally as the basis of their sentencing practice, and that studies of both judicial sentences and of parole point to the conclusion that offence gravity and criminal record are the major determining factors in sentencing, far and away more important in sentencing practice generally than are social factors. Nonetheless, how we react to this state of affairs will depend upon how robust the variable 'offence seriousness' proves to be. If judgments of offence seriousness are similar irrespective of age or social class — ideally if such judgments are similar throughout at least the Western world and over time — the variable 'offence seriousness' can be worked with for many practical purposes. If there are more modest levels of consensus, we would have to answer some awkward questions about what it is that the elite groups of judges and paroling authorities are using as their prime basis of handing down punishments, given that the perception of offence gravity is not something which they share with their fellow-citizens.

Consensus in judgments of offence seriousness

It is a strange paradox that the major study of crime seriousness, which is now regarded as the basis of the bulk of more recent work on the topic, is the one which was the least satisfactory in its treatment of the consensus issue. This was the investigation carried out by Thorsten Sellin and Marvin Wolfgang published in 1964 under the title *The Measurement of Delinquency*. It was more ambitious than earlier attempts to measure offence gravity judgments (Messedaglia, 1866; Mayr, 1867; Clark, 1922; Thurstone, 1927; Durea, 1933). Its authors state their major purposes in scaling offence seriousness as:

1. To select from multi-dimensional features of delinquency a single dimension, taking nto account the relative gravity or seriousness of delinquent acts;
2. To produce an empirical, objectively ascertained set of components of delinquency that would be examined by socially significant groups whose evaluations could be used as a basis for scoring:
3. To arrive at a system of weights for delinquent events for use in the construction of an index.

They selected 141 offences in the Philadelphia crime code varying systematically according to method used to inflict injury, the extent of injury, the value of property stolen or damaged, and whether intimidation had been used and by what means. Groups of university students, police officers and juvenile court judges were chosen to assess the seriousness of the offences. Sellin and Wolfgang concluded:

the seriousness of the crimes is evaluated in a similar way, without significant differences, by all the groups. The age of the offender does not particularly colour a person's judgement about the seriousness of the offence. A pervasive social agreement about what is serious and what is not appears to emerge and this agreement transcends simple qualitative concordance; it extends to the estimated numerical degree of seriousness of these offences.

However, Rose (1966) points out that the statistic on the basis of which Sellin and Wolfgang infer consensus, the similarity of slopes of regression lines, simply is not relevant to the decision as to consensus. Such similarity:

does not imply acceptance of the basic proposition. The factors which determine the relative seriousness of the offences rated are the order and spacing of points on the regression line and not merely the position of the line itself. Ten identical lines may therefore be generated by ten sets of points each with a completely different order and spacing.

The force of Rose's criticism, and the central position which the Sellin and Wolfgang research occupies among investigations of offence seriousness combine to produce a situation in which supporters of Sellin and Wolfgang (hereinafter the believers) and their opponents (the unbelievers) have tended to choose as their battleground the merits or otherwise of the Sellin and Wolfgang approach. This has served to divert attention from the resolution of the substantive issues with which the Sellin and Wolfgang research was concerned, such as whether there really is a consensus between social groups in the judgment of offence gravity. The believers seem to have been so preoccupied by responding to the detailed criticisms of Holy Writ (the published work of Sellin and Wolfgang) as to have eschewed its verification. The unbelievers have been so impatient of the obvious inadequacies of the Sellin and Wolfgang work as to fail to keep the important issues which they sought to illuminate in mind. Only occasionally has an unbeliever managed to keep the wood of purpose in sight among the trees of methodological detail. Walker (1971) provides the most elegant exposition of an unbeliever's position, although his root-and-branch dismissal of the desirability of measuring offence gravity is not the only tenable position, and is indeed not the position to be taken in this chapter.

Returning to the central issue, that of consensus as to judged offence seriousness, let us first be clear about what level of consensus we would find impressive. We would expect quite high levels of agreement at the group level as to the relative seriousness of general offence categories like murder, burglary and criminal damage. Agreement is likely to be imperfect for such mundane reasons as mistakes made, and also because of differences between people in the precise offence brought to mind by a particular offence description or title. For example, some people may judge rape to be more serious than murder because a particularly vicious rape may be imagined and contrasted with an image of a relatively 'clean' murder. Thus, even with single-word or phrase descriptions, consensus will be imperfect. The relevance of this imagining process to sentence is evident in the decision in *Kwok Yon Shing* [1968] Crim. L.R. 175. Here:

The offender was convicted of manslaughter on a charge of murder. The jury accepted by its verdict at least part of his evidence that his victim landlady had provoked him by unwanted sexual advances, threats to accuse him of indecency and threats to kill him. A sentence of twelve years was reduced to seven years. The original sentence was held to have been inconsistent with the view the jury must have taken.

We would expect less complete agreement as the number of different offences to be distinguished increases, and as the differences between offences thereby become more subtle. For this reason, high correlations between social groups would be particularly impressive when large number of offences are being rated.

Three types of consensus are of interest to us. They are consensus across time, between countries, and between social groups within a country. Some British evidence exists as to the last two types of agreement. To the writers' knowledge, the only evidence across time is American. Given that the Briton's stereotypical American is prone to more rather than less attitudinal volatility, one might suppose that consensus over time in judgments of crime seriousness is likely to be less in the United States than in the United Kingdom, and thus evidence of great agreement over time may be regarded as being particularly impressive if that evidence comes from across the North Atlantic. (We recognise the spuriousness of such reasoning based on national stereotypes. Our real position is that there is no obvious reason to suppose that consensus in judgments of offence seriousness across time will be lower in the United Kingdom than in the United States.) Thurstone (1927), in his pioneering attempt to scale offence seriousness, used 266 students at the University of Chicago. Offence descriptions were single words like kidnapping, adultery (*sic*) and arson. Thurstone's subjects generated a scale from rape and murder at the serious end through, in decreasing order of gravity, seduction, abortion, kidnapping, adultery, arson, perjury, embezzlement, counterfeiting, forgery, burglary, assault and battery, larceny, libel, smuggling, bootlegging and receiving stolen goods, to vagrancy as the least serious offence.

Forty years later, Clyde Coombs replicated the study with 369 students of the University of Michigan (1967). At the top end of the scale again were to be found murder and rape, and, in decreasing order of judged seriousness, kidnapping, arson, assault and battery, abortion, burglary, embezzlement, adultery, perjury, larceny, seduction, counterfeiting, forgery, smuggling, libel, receiving stolen goods, bootlegging and vagrancy. Although there are some changes, notably in the reduced seriousness of sexual 'offences' and bootlegging, the similarities between the two scales are much more impressive than the differences. To put it one way, for any pair of offences, there was a 94 per cent chance that their relative seriousness would be judged similarly in 1967 as it had been in 1927. A further replication ten years later (Krus and Sherman, 1977) showed only trivial changes from the Coombs study of 1967. As an interesting postscript to this series of studies, Carroll *et al.*)1974) repeated the study adding to the offences to be judged seven Watergate-related offences. The judged seriousness of Watergate crimes was exceeded only by those crimes which involved direct personal threat. This modified study should be repeated to see if the judged seriousness of Watergate crimes has declined.

The second type of consensus to be addressed is cross-cultural. The most extensive study to date is that of Professor André Normandeau 1970), reanalysed by Pease, Ireson and Thorpe (1975) (but see also Newman, 1976). Table 2 summarises the results. They are expressed as standardised scores by groups of students in the participating countries. It is clear that there is very substantial agreement between countries in judged offence seriousness, at least of the types of offence included. It is very regrettable that 'white collar' offences were not included, but the fact remains that in so far as consensus was looked for, it was found to exist cross-nationally. This is perhaps the more surprising when one considers how factors like the purchasing power of the dollar can affect matters by changing the perception of offences involving money as compared with other offences, and like the availability of hospital care, which determines how seriously you have to be wounded before hospitalisation becomes necessary.

Table 2 Standardised scores of offences seriousness[a] *(negative scores indicate offences rated as below median seriousness for the country concerned)*

	United States	Canada	England	Belgian Congo	China (Taiwan)	Indonesia	Brazil	Mexico
Theft of $1 (US)	−0·60	−0·54	−0·44	−0·19	−0·67	−0·75	−0·75	−0·89
Theft of $5	−0·60	−0·54	−0·44	−0·19	−0·67	−0·75	−0·75	−0·89
Theft of $20	−0·26	−0·54	−0·44	−0·19	−0·67	−0·75	−0·75	−0·89
Theft of $50	−0·26	−0·22	−0·44	0·04	−0·67	−0·75	−0·32	−0·49
Theft of $1,000	0·09	0·11	−0·24	0·48	0·17	0	0·11	−0·10
Theft of $5,000	0·43	0·75	0·15	2·27	0·17	0	0·54	0·69
Burglary $5	−0·26	−0·22	−0·24	0·04	0·17	0	−0·32	−0·49
Aggravated theft $5 (unarmed)	0·09	0·11	0·15	−0·19	0·17	0·75	0·11	0·30
Aggravated theft $5 (armed)	0·77	0·43	0·54	0·15	1·85	1·50	0·54	0·69
Assault (causing death)	7·91	8·14	9·34	12·78	5·21	5·25	5·25	5·44
Assault (necessitating hospital admission)	1·45	1·39	1·13	0·26	1·01	1·50	1·39	1·48
Assault (necessitating medical treatment, followed by discharge)	0·43	0·75	0·73	−0·07	0·17	0	0·54	0·30
Assault (minor)	−0·60	−0·22	0·15	−0·19	−0·67	−0·75	−0·32	−0·89
Rape	2·81	3·00	2·30	0·48	2·69	3·00	2·25	2·27
Theft of car (vehicle recovered undamaged)	−0·26	−0·22	−0·44	−0·19	−0·67	−0·75	−0·75	−0·89
Breaking and entering	−0·60	−0·54	−0·44	−0·07	−0·67	−0·75	−0·75	−0·89
Intimidation (involving verbal threats)	−0·26	−0·22	−0·05	−0·19	−0·67	0	−0·32	−0·10
Intimidation (involving weapon)	0·43	0·11	0·34	0·04	1·01	0·75	2·25	0·30

Notes: 'Aggravated theft' = theft involving violence.

'Burglary 5 dollars' = breaking and entering and stealing $5

'Assault' = involving physical force

(a) Standardised scores are scores adjusted, in this case, so that overall average (median) seriousness for each country is 0, and dispersion is similarly made equivalent across countries. Negative scores indicate a seriousness rating for the offence lower than the average for that country, and positive scores higher than the average. Identical scores represent identically extreme judgements, relative to all judgements made.

Table reprinted by special permission of the *Journal of Criminal Law and Criminology*, © Northwestern University School of Law, Vol. 66, No. 2.

Consensus of offence-seriousness judgments across time and nations gives reason for hope that similar agreement exists between groups within a society. A variety of studies have found this to be the case, in cultures as diverse as Canada (Akman *et al.*, 1967) and Puerto Rico (Velez-Diaz and Megargee, 1970). However the most thorough work of this kind has perhaps been that of Rossi *et al.* (1974). They used a representative sample of 200 adults in Baltimore in 1972, whom they asked to rate 140 offences according to how serious they believed the acts described to be. Dividing the group according to race, education and sex, they found that judgments of offence seriousness were highly similar as between races, sexes and levels of education. Looking at combinations of these factors, it was found that black males with less than high-school education constituted the group which exhibited least agreement with other groups. Even here, the correlation of seriousness judgments with other groups was high and positive, and:

the main points of disagreement centre around [*sic*] certain crimes against the person, particularly those in which the offender and the victim are known to each other. For example, compared to the total sample, 'beating up an acquaintance' is regarded much less seriously by poorly educated black males. The line between manly sport and crime can be thin indeed.

Rossi and his colleagues carry out some interesting supplementary analyses. For example, if you had to choose a group in terms of, say, age and education, whose views of offence seriousness corresponded most closely to those of the adult population at large, which group would you choose? Perhaps you would choose the old and poorly educated, on the grounds that their age gives them more time in which to have absorbed the culture's norms of offence seriousness, and their poor education fails to make them aware of the full range of circumstances and possible subcultural relativities surrounding offences. If that would have been your prediction, as in honesty it would have been ours, it would have been wrong. The group which most accurately reflects the population's views comprises the young and highly educated. Rossi *et al.* suggest that 'exposure to the normative structure and language-handling ability lead to better knowledge of the normative structure'. This has all the hallmarks of a half-hearted *post hoc* account. It is not youth's superior knowledge of the normative structure which was demonstrated, it is youth's greater acceptance of the normative structure. It may simply be untrue that the young and well educated know better the relative wrongness of things. They may simply accept more fully that which they know. Whatever the reason for Rossi *et al*'s interesting results, it is difficult to escape the implication that the judges who would most faithfully reflect the values of society in their sentencing practice would be young ones!

British research on social consensus in judgments of offence seriousness exists, although it is perhaps not as thoroughgoing as the work of Rossi and his colleagues. The only pieces of work based on representative samples are those of Walker (1978) and of Durant *et al*. (1972). The latter study gathered responses from a sample of 1,904 adults to questions about eighteen offences. Unfortunately for purposes of comparison, people were simply asked to judge offences as serious or not serious rather than to rank or score their seriousness. People will obviously differ in their threshold of what is regarded as serious even when they agree on a ranking of seriousness. However, the proportion of people judging an offence to be serious may itself be taken as a rough indication of judges seriousness, and the scale thus generated, reproduced here as Table 3, is recognisably similar to the other rankings of offence seriousness to be found in this chapter. This found, we can have more confidence in Table 4, which shows the perception of seriousness by socio-economic group, and in Table 5, which breaks down the same data by age. By both age and social class, the degree of agreement in the judgment of offence seriousness is remarkable. A similarly remarkable coincidence of judgment is found between the general population and people in Borstals, detention centres and prisons, and between city, town and country dwellers, and between people who had admitted to the commission of particular offences and those who had not. Following the scent laid down by Rossi and his co-workers, we wished to discover which group most faithfully mimics the general population in terms of judgments of offence seriousness. We correlated seriousness scores from each social group with that from the total population. Unfortunately the education variable was simply dichotomised into 'higher' and 'lower' and its analysis would not have proved illuminating. We found no difference between age groups or between social classes in the level of correlation with overall judgments of offence seriousness. All correlations were almost perfect. Thus, from this crude secondary analysis, we are left with no evidence for discernible class or age normative differences in judgments of offence seriousness.

Table 3 *Seriousness of offences, judgments of representative English sample (%);*
N = 1,904

Offence	Serious	Not Serious
Murder	99	_a
Robbery with violence	99	1
Committing a sexual offence against a child under 13 years	98	1
Cruelty to children	98	2
Indecently assaulting a woman	96	4
Causing death by dangerous driving	94	6
Manslaughter	86	14
Deliberately damaging property	69	29
Fraud (that is, obtaining money by false pretences)	64	35
Housebreaking	61	38
Breaking into a factory	46	54
Stealing (without violence)	33	66
Fighting (sometimes known as common assault)	30	69
Taking away a motor vehicle (without the owner's consent, but *not* intending to steal it)	24	76
Being drunk and disorderly	19	81
Stealing by finding	13	86
Travelling on a bus, train, etc. without paying the fare	10	89
Vagrancy (living rough with no fixed home or proper means of support)	10	90

Note:
(a) Less than 0·5 per cent.
Source: Durant *et al.*, 1972.

Walker (1978) gave a random sample of 475 citizens of Sheffield eleven offences to judge in terms of their gravity. Comparing sexes and social classes, she found that 'the rank correlation between groups was high. Those between males and females for the three social groups and those between pairs of social groups for males and females separately, all exceeded 0·86.' Thus the story of high consensus continues, although Walker did come across social-class differences, people in the lower social classes rating income tax evasion as more serious, and violence as less serious, than did higher social classes. Interestingly, members of lower social classes also judged crimes as generally more serious. This may be a trivial class difference in the way in which numbers are used, or a more profound one in terms of distaste for crime in general.

Table 4   *Proportion regarding certain offences as serious, analysed by socio-economic status and by level of education (%)*

Base of %: all informants	Total 1,904	High 1 97	2 158	3 434	4 401	Low 5 328	Education Higher 409	Lower 1,489
Murder	99	100	99	99	99	99	100	99
Robbery with violence	99	100	98	99	99	97	99	98
Committing a sexual offence against a child after 13 years	98	98	99	98	99	98	99	93
Cruelty to children	98	99	98	98	97	97	98	97
Indecently assaulting a woman	96	99	96	96	95	93	98	95
Causing a death by dangerous driving	94	96	92	95	94	92	97	93
Manslaughter	86	89	83	89	83	83	87	85
Deliberately damaging property	69	66	65	73	67	69	72	68
Fraud	64	64	61	69	61	62	68	63
Housebreaking	61	62	61	64	61	61	63	60
Breaking into a factory	46	50	42	52	42	45	51	44
Stealing (without violence)	33	50	30	38	32	26	45	30
Fighting (common assault)	30	26	27	30	29	32	25	32
Taking away a motor vehicle without owner's consent	24	24	18	24	27	29	25	23
Being drunk and disorderly	19	16	14	19	18	21	13	20
Stealing by finding	13	9	14	12	13	14	15	13
Travelling on a bus, train etc. without paying the fare	10	8	7	10	8	14	10	10
Vagrancy	10	4	8	8	10	13	5	11

Source: Durant *et al.*, 1972.

Sparks *et al.* (1977), in their victim survey, were also concerned with consensus across class in judgments of offence seriousness. They asked 537 respondents in three areas of London to score offences as to their gravity. They found that 'While the rank orders of these mean scores differ to some extent ... there is still a substantial amount of agreement between different social classes. Even between classes I and V, the rank correlation of the order of mean scores is 0·706, which is certainly highly significant.' The major difference according to social class was that:

for lower-class respondents, there tends to be less difference between scores given to offences of violence, and scores given to offences against property, than is the case for upper-class respondents; in other words, relative to the

Table 5 *Proportion regarding certain offences as serious, analysed by age (%)*

		Age			
Base of %: all informants	Total 1904	21–30 317	31–40 417	41–50 454	51–69 712
Murder	99	99	99	100	99
Robbery with violence	99	100	99	100	97
Committing a sexual offence against a child under 13 years	98	99	99	99	98
Cruelty to children	98	98	99	98	96
Indecently assaulting a woman	96	93	95	97	96
Causing death by dangerous driving	94	94	95	94	93
Manslaughter	86	88	88	85	84
Deliberately damaging property	69	69	68	69	70
Fraud	64	66	68	64	62
Housebreaking	61	55	62	62	62
Breaking into a factory	46	47	44	47	45
Stealing (without violence)	33	34	37	35	29
Fighting (common assault)	30	26	33	29	31
Taking away a motor vehicle without owner's consent	24	18	26	26	24
Being drunk and disorderly	19	15	12	23	21
Stealing by finding	13	10	12	15	14
Travelling on a bus, train etc. without paying the fare	10	8	9	10	12
Vagrancy	10	11	9	8	10

Source: Durant *et al.*, 1972.

generally similar scores which they gave to violent offences, the lower-class respondent gave higher scores to property crimes than the middle-class ones did.

One is tempted to seek an explanation for this pattern along lines familiar to the reader from the discussion of the cross-cultural data earlier, namely that money amounts must not be thought of as fixed sums, but as potential goods, in terms of what that money will buy in relation to what one already owns. Looked at in this light, property offences are almost bound to be seen as more serious by those who possess less.

A study of magistrates' ranking of offences was undertaken by Hood (1972). He found significant consensus in the ranking of the seriousness of offences, and within-offence ranking of offence descriptions. There was a significant association between a magistrate's ranking of an offence's seriousness and the penalty he chose as appropriate.

A study by Pease *et al.* (1976) describes an attempt to develop a scale of offence seriousness. They found that correlations in the ranking of the gravity of crimes was very high as between groups of students, probation officers, clerks and magistrates. In a different approach from the ones adopted earlier they set out to develop a scale of offence seriousness such that a minimum of 70 per cent of people would agree about the relative seriousness of *each adjacent pair* of offences. The scale satisfying this condition is reproduced as Table 6. Given that a range of actual events can be encompassed by each of the offence descriptions, and that any of the possible offences can be imagined by the respondent, it is remarkable that a scale of such length satisfying the 70 per cent agreement condition can be generated. In fact the scale, although it has a minimum value of 70 per cent agreement between adjacent offences, in fact has an average level of agreement between adjacent items which is as high as 83 per cent. The level of consensus revealed in this study is thus, as in the others reported, very high.

The only study seriously to question the widespread consensus on offence seriousness between social groups on empirical grounds is that of Lesieur and Lehman (1975). They concluded, 'It appears questionable whether "seriousness" is scalable at all, and, if it is scalable whether it is a unidimensional phenomenon.' The results of the Lesieur and Lehman study diverge so widely from those of other studies that it is difficult to understand what can have produced such a dramatic contrast. Certainly the study should be repeated, but, until that is done and the results are confirmed, the overwhelming weight of evidence favours widespread consensus as to offence seriousness judgments. Another study (Sherman and Dowdle, 1974) conceded consensus but suggested that variables underlying punishment choice are not reducible to a single seriousness dimension.

In summary, then, we would assert that on almost every occasion that consensus of judgments of offence gravity has been sought, across time, between cultures and among social groups, it has been found in remarkably large measure. There are obvious reasons why

Table 6   *Scale of offence seriousness with minimum 70 per cent agreement as to relative seriousness of adjacent items (average agreement between adjacent items = 83 per cent)*

(a)   The offender robs a person at gunpoint. The victim struggles and is shot to death.

(b)   The offender kills a person by driving a car recklessly.

(c)   The offender wounds a person with a blunt instrument. The victim lives but requires hospitalisation.

(d)   The offender, armed with a blunt instrument, robs a person of £500. The victim is wounded and requires treatment by a doctor but no further treatment is required.

(e)   A victim is robbed of £2 by an offender armed with a blunt instrument. The victim is wounded and requires treatment by a doctor but no further treatment is needed.

(f)   The offender, using physical force, robs a person of £2. The victim is hurt and requires treatment by a doctor but no further treatment is required.

(g)   The offender, armed with a blunt instrument, robs a victim of £2. The victim is not hurt.

(h)   The offender breaks into a school and takes equipment worth £500.

(i)   The offender picks a person's pocket of £500.

(j)   The offender steals an unlocked car and abandons but does not damage it.

(k)   The offender steals an unlocked car and returns it undamaged to the place from where it was stolen.

(l)   The offender throws stones through windows.

(m)   The offender is drunk and disorderly in public.

(n)   The offender disturbs the neighbourhood with loud, noisy behaviour.

the consensus is not likely to be complete, but it is certainly enough to encourage the recognition of the dimension as basic and comprehensible. Perhaps the most remarkable consensus of all has not been mentioned up to this point — the consensus among people who are asked to assign seriousness scores to descriptions of crimes that it is a sensible and meaningful task for them. Walker (1978) evinced some disapproval of the term 'offence seriousness'. She wrote, 'The concept of the seriousness of an offence is vague and ill-defined and may depend upon the description of the offence and the context in which the subject is asked to judge. Different social classes may attach different meanings to the word "serious"; some may judge it morally and others in terms of loss to the victim.' Nonetheless, it will be recalled that, with exceptions, Walker found high consensus in the judgment of offence seriousness. She also concluded, most interestingly in the light of her earlier scepticism, that 'this study has shown that members of the general population are able to assess numerically the relative seriousness of a set of offences in three different ways in so consistent a manner that it must be concluded that this is a meaningful operation for them.'

How do people judge seriousness?

Psychological research has shown us that no perception is basic, that each is constructed from a set of sense elements. As you read this page, you are not aware of the black holes in your visual field which are your optic discs. It is therefore not sensible to contrast the naturalness and immediacy of the perception of physical properties like shape and colour with the artificiality of social perceptions like offence seriousness. In both cases, the final perception or judgment is the end point of a complex interpretive process. Nonetheless we may safely base everyday decisions upon our perceptions of shape and colour, using these features of the segments of a dartboard to exercise our skill at the game. Similarly, it seems, we can base everyday decisions about approval, disapproval and punishment on the largely agreed dimension of offence seriousness. Notwithstanding our capacity to use the dimension, we should attempt an analysis of features associated with the perception of offence seriousness in just the same way as experimental psychologists have attempted to analyse the mechanisms of other perceptual systems. Rossi *et al.* (1974) developed a crime classification system, and then assessed how serious crimes in the various categories were judged to be. It was clear that extent of injury inflicted and amount of monetary loss incurred were both relevant, in the intuitively obvious direction, in determining judged seriousness. The involvement of drugs and the violation of public order in the course of an offence also served to boost levels of judged seriousness, as did the involvement of the state as victim (as in spying). These are perhaps results which could have been anticipated (although the 'knew-it-all-along' effect described in Chapter 2 should reduce our confidence in our retrospective accuracy).

This type of analysis takes us only slightly further in our search for the basis of judged offence seriousness. It helps us to identify the factors which are relevant, but not how they are used in combination to yield a score of offence seriousness. This issue of combination is without doubt a matter of some difficulty. Indeed, there is a suggestion that the conventional ways of generating judgments of offence seriousness may give misleading results in this respect. Bryant *et al.* (1968) criticise the method whereby people simply assign numbers to events in proportion to their judged seriousness. They opined: 'The crime scales derived in these studies ... appear to be unreasonably compressed, in the sense that the ratings for serious and slight crimes seem closer together than intuition would lead one to suspect, and this suggests that the rating methods used perhaps suffer from some basic shortcomings.' Their own studies with policemen:

led us to the important conclusion that despite the instructions given to the subjects, the ratings obtained (by the type of method used by Sellin and Wolfgang) simply do not reflect the subjects' judgements on a ratio scale. Thus, for example, if a subject scores the value of preventing one crime A at 30 and another crime B at 10, our experience is that, if questioned, the subject will usually express a preference for preventing one crime of type A rather than say four (or more) crimes of type B, and further that if the subject is confronted with this inconsistency, he will almost invariably amend his scores rather than the preference statement.

It will be recalled that Bryant *et al.* preferred statements about offence prevention and detection to statements about seriousness, but that the judgments appeared to be equivalent to seriousness judgments in the way in which people used them.

It may well be that the point made by Bryant *et al.* is correct, that people forced to make preference statements do so in ways which reveal that the conventional methods of measuring seriousness (notably magnitude estimation) are flawed. Alternatively, it may be that preference statements are less suited to judgments of seriousness than are magnitude estimations. Perhaps the police officers questioned by Bryant *et al.* were forced into judgments of something other than offence seriousness by the form of the preference statement, which would lead to the conclusion that Sellin and Wolfgang's method was sound. Be that as it may, the reader should not lose sight of the fact that sentences are in real life pronounced in terms of magnitude estimation, not in terms of preference statements. If seriousness judgments are flawed in the way suggested, so will be sentences themselves. If we follow this line of thought, we may conclude that sentences should be couched in terms of preference statements of the kind favoured by Bryant *et al.* Alternatively, it may mean that retributive sentencing is less readily embodied in statements of preferred outcomes, just like judgments of offence seriousness.

The work of Bryant and his colleagues at Lancaster University was developed by Aspden (1971). He generated an optimal police deployment pattern from data which included policemen's judgments of detection and prevention values (effectively, as we have seen, offence seriousness). In Aspden's optimal deployment pattern, the estimated number of traffic offences which would be detected increased much more than other types of offence. That is to say, given the value weightings assigned to the different types of offence, it was traffic offences which contributed a disproportionately large amount of the additional effectiveness resulting from Aspden's optimal deployment pattern. This 'optimal' solution was rejected both by Aspden and by the police he was dealing with. It appears that the value which the police give to the detection of a traffic offence is specific to a particular rate of detection. Aspden's general argument is that the more traffic offences currently detected, the lower the value assigned to the detection of an extra one. If that is so, it seems that detection rate operates directly on the assessed seriousness of an offence.

Young (1971), writing about marijuana-users, seems to imply that the same rule of diminishing returns applies, with the result that the police 'contain the problem rather than ... eliminate it'. Arrests for being drunk and disorderly and for minor sexual offences may well be characterised by the same value diminution. This hypothesised rule of diminishing returns operating directly on judgments of offence seriousness is crucial for an understanding of those judgments. It implies a 'size of social problem' underpinning for such judgments, with the same act being judged differently at different times depending upon its prevalence, detected and undetected. This fits neatly with the difficulty, referred to earlier, of distinguishing deterrent sentencing from harsh retributive sentencing. If 'size of social problem' feeds directly into judgments of offence seriousness, deterrent sentencing and harsh retributive sentencing are almost inevitably indistinguishable, because offences judged to represent a social problem are *ipso facto* judged grave. To coin a phrase, further research is necessary.

The Gottfredson family is to American criminology what the Kennedy family is to American politics, although thankfully less star-crossed. The work of Don Gottfredson has already been mentioned, and that of one of his criminologist sons, Stephen, substantially illuminates the bases of judgments of offence seriousness (Gottfredson *et al.* 1980). They had students judge the seriousness of five crime types. Each crime description was kept simple, and for each crime type ten variants were generated, according to the amount of monetary loss incurred. Thus each of the five crime types − burglary, cheque fraud, robbery, theft and rape − was linked to each of the ten degrees of monetary loss, from $5 to $10,000. The aspect of the study which is of interest here is whether people mentally calculate offence seriousness by, as it were, adding a constant extra seriousness score for every extra dollar involved in each offence. The answer is that they did not. The amount of money stolen during a rape had little effect on the judged seriousness of rape, some slight effect on the judged seriousness of robbery, and the greatest effect on the other offences, with the maximum effect on the judged seriousness of cheque frauds. The results make it clear that money value subtly, rather than mechanically, affects judged seriousness. Where extent of gain can be perfectly foreseen, as in cheque fraud, dollar value is highly relevant to judged seriousness. Where it can be at best imperfectly foreseen, as in rape and robbery, it is much less relevant (although never entirely irrelevant).

To this point, we have seen that amount of loss, damage and injury operate directly (but not mechanically) on judgments of offence seriousness. We have speculated, on the basis of slight evidence, that offence prevalence operates directly on judgments of offence seriousness. Are there any other factors which operate directly on such judgments? The obvious candidate is the perception of the offender. Answering the question as to whether offender characteristics directly impact on perceived offence seriousness is crucial for an understanding of sentencing in general and mitigation in particular. Is mitigation an induced reduction of the horror of the crime as imagined, or does it operate on the perception of the offender while leaving the judged heinousness of the offence unchanged? The first alternative is not always implausible. To take the most emotive example possible, is an imagined rape by a first offender with a good work record who has suffered a recent bereavement seen as clumsy and sad rather than skilled and callous? What happens when details of the offender are added to the details of the offence needed to maximise consensus in seriousness judgments (Christiansen *et al.*, 1970)? If the addition makes no difference, it means that mitigation probably operates in the second of the two ways distinguished above. It means that the two dimensions argued to underlie sentencing, offence gravity and offender record, are independent on the basis of research, as the work of Leslie Wilkins and his colleagues suggested. If, on the other hand, information about the offender changes the judgment of the seriousness of his offence, then all this is called into question. It will be clear to the reader which of the alternatives we would prefer.

However, if the reader feels as we did on confronting the issue, he will predict that in fact description of offender characteristics will influence assessed offence seriousness. One of us is on record as holding that view (Pease *et al.* 1976). But there are now two pieces of evidence which suggest that our presupposition is wrong and that information about the offender does not influence assessments of offence seriousness (Reidel, 1975; Walker, 1978). Monica Walker gave a standard description of an offender to each person subjected to the study referred to earlier. People were given 'one of two different offender descriptions: (1) the man is English; aged 28, he is married with no children; he has no previous convictions; he has a University degree; he is a technician in a research department of an industrial firm; (2) the same as above for the first four items; he left school at 15; he is a builder's labourer.' She concluded:

no significant differences were found between the scores for subjects given the different types for any of the offences. This was, perhaps, particularly surprising for the two offences where there were overall social class differences – violence and income tax evasion. It might have been expected that these offences would have been regarded as more or less serious in relation to the type of offender, at least by some social grades.

More extensive data of the same type, albeit from a sample un-representative of the general population, was gathered by Reidel (1975). Thus, to our astonishment, people can make judgments of offence seriousness uncontaminated by considerations of who the offender is.

The metric of offence seriousness

Questions which sound academic often yield answers whose practical implications are profound. So it is here. The academic-sounding question is: can you do arithmetic on judgments of offence serious-ness? This apparently vacuous question is in fact central to an under-standing of the role of judgments of offence seriousness in sentencing practice. Its consideration here is therefore intrinsically worthwhile, and it additionally provides a bridge from this chapter into an analysis of the concept of proportionality in sentencing which is dealt with in Chapter 6.

Sellin and Wolfgang (1964) assert that you can do arithmetic on seriousness judgments. They imply that people judge how serious an offence is by mentally adding together the seriousness scores they would assign to the offence elements. Thus, if a person gives a seriousness score of 10 to rape and 20 to murder, the assumption is that he will give a seriousness score of 30 to the offence of rape plus murder. Our examination of the work of Gottfredson *et al.* (1980) has already shown that this is not so, even if intuition were not sufficient to reach this conclusion (but a theme of this book is that intuition is often unreliable).

However, is the position the same with separate offences? For example Sellin and Wolfgang wrote, 'If two robbery events occur, each of which has intimidation of one victim by an offender without a weapon and each of which is a 3 dollar theft, the score for each offence is 2 for intimidation plus 1 for money loss or a total of 3; and the two events total 6.' Gottfredson *et al.* (1980) showed that arithmetic within the offence event was misguided. Pease *et al.* (1974) showed that arithmetic across events was misguided. They asked people to judge whether committing two identical events within a short time was more than twice as serious, twice as serious, or less than twice as serious as committing one such offence. On the basis of the Sellin and Wolfgang assumption, the conclusion that they should judge it as exactly twice as serious is inescapable. In the Pease *et al.* (1974) experiment, only 32 per cent of judgments conformed to the Sellin and Wolfgang prediction. The study was criticised by Wellford and Wiatrowski (1975) but replication after removing the alleged methodological shortcoming produced essentially the same results (Wagner and Pease, 1978). Thus it is clear that across offences, as for elements within individual offences, offence gravity is not a variable on which you can sensibly do sums. This is perhaps consistent with the practice of the Court of Appeal in reducing aggregate sentences when there are consecutive terms, each term in itself being judged correct.

In the case of *Vickers* ([1974] Crim. L.R. 56),

the offender aged 27 pleaded guilty to robbery and inflicting grievous bodily harm. He asked for two offences of robbery to be taken into account. In 1970 he tripped up an 80 years old woman in a street and snatched her handbag.

He also snatched the handbags of two other women. In 1972 he hit his father-in-law during a quarrel, breaking his cheek bone. He was sentenced to six years' imprisonment: four years for robbery and two years consecutive for assault. He had two previous convictions for theft and had been fined and sentenced to six months' imprisonment suspended. He had not served a prison sentence. Though robbery were present and the assault was unpleasant and serious and though the sentences were proper when looked at separately the Court of Appeal held that the total was too much and ordered the sentences to run concurrently.

And in the case of *Koyce* ((1979) 1 Cr. App. Rep. (S), 21) we read: 'A sentencer who imposes a series of consecutive terms of imprisonment should review the aggregate ... and reduce it if it appears that the total sentence is excessive, notwithstanding that the individual component sentences are correct and the offences are unrelated.' The court in taking that view is explicitly (although obviously not consciously) rejecting the hypothesis that offence seriousness is additive.

CHAPTER 6

The scaling of penal pain

In the last fifteen years, there has been a marked shift within academic criminology (not necessarily reflected in the practices of decision-makers in the criminal justice system) from the advocacy of reductive sentencing, based primarily on the rehabilitative purpose, to advocacy of retributive or 'just deserts' sentencing. The reasons from the change partly derive from criminological research but to a greater extent from reasons of principle. The two bases for the shift should be briefly described in order to justify the emphasis on retributive purpose in this and the following chapter.

The reason for a movement away from the principle of reductive sentencing which derives from criminological research is that evidence suggests one should not be confident of the easy achievement of the intended reduction. However much the reducer wants to reduce crime, it is clear that the extent to which he can do it through the penal system is limited. Despite the fact that their conclusions were somewhat overstated, the large literature reviews of the mid-1970s (Lipton *et al.*, 1974; Brody, 1976) certainly dispelled the notion that the purpose of reduction was easy of attainment. The painstaking work of Beyleveld (1978) suggests that deterrence is an infinitely complex process. The factors of certainty of detection of offence, severity of sentence and communication of sentence choice are all relevant to a consideration of deterrent effects, and the bulk of the available evidence is not easy to interpret as indicative of a strong deterrent effect of current penal practice.

Thirdly, evidence that the criminal justice system prevents a lot of crime simply by keeping people out of circulation is difficult to reconcile with the general run of estimates of the incapacitative effects of imprisonment (Van Dine *et al.*, 1977; Cohen, 1978), although the interpretation of these data should be attended by caution (see Pease and Wolfson, 1979; Ainsworth and Pease, 1981) and is subject to change on the basis of the study of criminal careers (Petersilia, 1980). All the foregoing suggests that, for the foreseeable future, one is right to be pessimistic about the reliable translation of a sentencer's crime-reductive intention into the actual reduction of crime.

The thrust of the attack of principle on reductive sentencing is directed almost exclusively towards the rehabilitative intention (see for example Bottomley, 1980). What is objectionable, it is generally argued, is that in practice rehabilitation takes on a different reality, namely one where control over the individual is extended in the name of welfare.

The new therapeutic state has from the beginning contained mixed strains of both social defence and individual welfare, carrying out programmes of confinement and compulsory therapy which could not be justified by considerations other than those of social defence, yet relying upon its manifest dedication to welfare in order to combat criticisms of its disregard for the traditional safeguard of the criminal process. (Kittrie 1971).

In similar vein: 'Under the dominance of the rehabilitative ideal, the language of therapy is frequently employed, wittingly or unwittingly, to disguise the true state of affairs that prevails in our custodial institutions and at other points in the correctional process' (Allen, 1959). Thereby the notion of rehabilitation is held to justify lengths or types of treatment in institutions that could not otherwise be justified. Concerning juveniles, Allen (1964) writes: 'It is, in my judgement, both inaccurate and deceptive to describe the operation of the juvenile court in this area as the exercise of a rehabilitative or therapeutic function ... The primary function being served in these cases ... is the temporary incapacitation of children found to constitute a threat to the community's interest.' In the United Kingdom, one could use as an example the operation of children's hearings in Scotland, whereby disposals that were in intent therapeutic are used by Sheriffs in adult courts as part of the criminal history which will serve to make more severe the sentence passed. One may also observe in parole a system whose rhetoric is (in part) based on treatment but at least part of whose reality is the facilitation of institutional control.

A second difficulty with the rehabilitative ideal is that it diverts attention from the nature and causes of crime. For example, how would we regard attempts at the rehabilitation of witches? Treating witches stops you examining your assumptions about witchcraft. Attempting to rehabilitate homosexual people stops you examining your assumptions about normal sexuality. On a different level, one could argue that attempting to rehabilitate juvenile takers of motor vehicles diverts attention from the pitiful levels of car security effected by the manufacturer.

These difficulties of principle would perhaps have remained in the background had rehabilitation been found to be easy. A lot might have been forgiven, perhaps, if the penal system actually stopped burglars being burglars, rapists being rapists, and witches being witches. But, as stated earlier, the empirical evidence suggests we have a long way to go before achieving predictable and powerful change.

Particular targets of those criticising the rehabilitative aspect of reductivism have been the juvenile justice system (e.g. Lemert, 1970), parole (Hood, 1974) and to a lesser extent the sentencing of adults (Von Hirsch, 1976). The last named in particular advocates the substitution of reductive sentencing by retribution. He advocates the principle of commensurate deserts, that 'severity of punishment should be commensurate with the seriousness of the wrong', and develops the principle as follows:

The commensurate deserts principle may sometimes conflict with other objectives ... We think the commensurate deserts principle should have priority over other objectives in decisions about how much to punish. The disposition of convicted offenders should be commensurate with the seriousness of their offences, even if greater or less severity would promote other goals. For the principle, we have argued, is a principle of justice, whereas deterrence, incapacitation and rehabilitation are essentially strategies for controlling crime.

Although psychological study of judicial decision-making in general has been limited, it is especially paradoxical that the ascendant penal philosophy has had effectively no research attention. Apart from brief articles by McFatter (1978) and Farrington (1978), the present writers are unaware of attempts even to suggest how to address empirically the evaluation of the extent to which the aim of retribution in sentencing is satisfied.

Proportion is a word much used in texts on judicial sentencing. Pugsley (1979) argues for 'a straightforward matching of ... penalties to the perceived severity ... of offence'. Cross (1975) wrote, 'How much punishment should be inflicted? The answer is: as much as is deserved for the offence, no more, no less ... The general rule is one of proportionality.' The Streatfeild Report (1961) describes the tariff system as one whose 'primary objective was to fix a sentence proportionate to the offender's culpability.' Thomas (1979a) tells of sentences in the tariff system as intended to 'reflect the offender's culpability'. Gross (1979) makes the point most strongly: 'This general principle of proportionality between crime and punishment is a principle of just desert that serves as the justification of every criminal sentence that is justifiable.'

The goal of retributive sentencing, therefore, is proportionality. For the fully responsible actor, culpability is equivalent to seriousness of crime. For him, the goal is proportionality between offence seriousness and sentence severity. However, the nature of the proportionality link is not specified. There can be an infinite number of different proportionalities. One general set of proportionalities has one variable (for example, weight) going up as the other variable goes down (life expectancy). In another set, the variables both increase. Within each set, the rates of change of the variables generate different proportionalities. To talk of proportionality as though it actually prescribed sentencing behaviour is not helpful. The situation resembles that of the manufacturer of several models of car who publishes a common instruction book stating that running-in speed should be proportional to engine capacity. The instruction book also tells you the engine capacity of each model and leaves it at that. Although one can make a fair guess that the bigger the engine the higher the running-in speed should be, the individual owner would still not know how best to drive his car. Similarly in sentencing, although the proportion to which Pugsley and the others allude is certainly one in which sentences increase as culpability increases, the precise relationship is left for individual judges to decide. Choice in both cases can have serious implications. A car run in too fast may deteriorate quickly, and the lack of a specifiable proportional relationship between offence and sentence leaves room for disparity in sentencing and consequent injustice.

For us, at this stage, the question was whether there existed a means of investigating the proportionality link between offence and sentencing which would enable a more informed discussion of sentencing practice. We turned to psychophysics, that branch of experimental psychology concerned with the study of man as a measuring instrument. Throughout the history of psychophysics, four main functions have traditionally related physical to psychological magnitude. Of these (linear, logarithmic, exponential and power functions), the last most appealed to us. Still known by the name of its originator, Stevens' power function is one of the best known principles in psychophysics. It can be written as $\psi = k\phi^\beta$, in which the psychological (sensation) magnitude ψ grows as a power function of the stimulus magnitude ϕ. The exponent β, the 'signature' of the relationship, reflects the relative rate of increase along the two scales, k being a constant. In this sense, it embodies the proportionality link between the two variables. The power function indicates that a linear increase along the stimulus scale corresponds to a geometric increase along the response scale or, as Stevens (1975) argues, represents a relation where 'equal stimulus ratios produce equal subjective ratios'. Another facet of the power law is the way in which it describes, when transformed to logarithms, a straight line relating two variables with β as the slope of the line. So from $\psi = \psi\phi^\beta$ we get log $\psi = \beta\log\phi + \log k$.

Thus expressed, the differences in proportionalities are differences in slope. In terms of a discussion of seriousness and sentence length, the power function has definite advantages:

(1) The power function has been verified for hundreds of psychological continua (Stevens, 1975). Although theoretically limited to measurements as ratio level, it has been shown to be applicable to measurements at other levels (Stevens, 1971).

(2) The psychophysical measurement of social variables has been historically associated with the power function. In particular, the measurement of offence seriousness was treated in this manner by Sellin and Wolfgang (1964).

(3) The task known as cross-modality matching involving the matching of scores from two psychological variables has been associated with the work of Stevens on the power function. The allocation of sentence length to offence seriousness is in essence a cross-modality matching exercise.

(4) The logarithmic transformation of data flows from the assumption of a power relationship and invariably yields a straight line when the actual relationship is monotonic. This is convenient both for our purposes and for our conceivable use of this type of analysis in monitoring judicial performance.

Thus we chose the power function. Substituting our terms in the relevant formula, we have:

log sentence length $= \beta$ log offence seriousness $+$ log k.

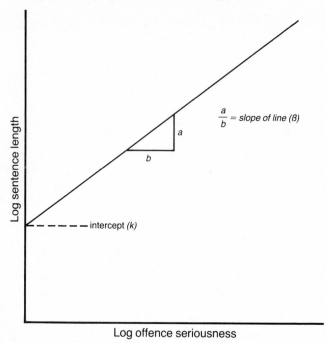

Figure 1   Schematic representation of relationship between sentence length and offence seriousness

The term which enshrines the proportionality link between the variables is β. Figure 1 gives a schematic representation of the relationship of interest, together with relevant terms.

A pilot study of proportionality in sentencing

Having decided on both the variables and the mode of analysis, we engaged in an exploratory study of proportionality in sentencing. At the University of Manchester, forty-one undergraduates were presented with twelve case descriptions. All such descriptions were of rape cases, and the cases varied systematically in terms of the physical harm inflicted on the victim, the prior relationship between rapist and victim, and the age of the victim. It was assumed that these variables were relevant to judgments of offence seriousness. Each subject had to assign an offence seriousness score to each case and to indicate an appropriate length of prison sentence. The order of the two tasks was varied so that the scaling of the variables against each other could not be an artefact of the order of presentation. For each of the twelve cases the log of mean sentence length and log of geometric mean magnitude estimate of offence seriousness were calculated and plotted. Logarithms were used since, it will be recalled, the logarithms of data points in a monotonic function form a straight line whose slope is the exponent β of the power relationship (Stevens, 1975). In our data, the coefficient of determination $R^2 = 0 \cdot 85$. This represents the proportion of variation in sentence length accountable for by variation in offence seriousness. It can vary from 0 to 1. In the latter extreme case, all variation in sentence length would be accounted for by variation in offence seriousness.

The slope (exponent) represents the kind of proportionality linking the variables of offence seriousness and sentence length. If the exponent were 1, this would mean that doubling offence seriousness doubles sentence length. The exponent was in fact $0 \cdot 73$. This means that a doubling of offence seriousness less than doubles sentence length, and tells precisely by how much.

In terms of justice, should the exponent be more than, less than or equal to 1? The exponent of one *exactly* could attract support. The exponent of less than one also has a case for being regarded as reasonable. The hypothesis for the latter is that severity of sentence operates as a mediating variable between offence seriousness and sentence length. Sentence severity, it could be argued, would increase faster than sentence length because of the problems associated with long custodial sentences − difficulties of resettlement, dissolution of social ties, age and so on. It is interesting that Ashworth (1984) has extrapolated a scale of punishments from a 'guideline' judgment of Lord Chief Justice Lane. It relates street value of a drug consignment to proper sentence. It runs as follows:

£100,000	7 years
£250,000	8 years
£400,000	9 years
£550,000	10 years
£700,000	11 years
£850,000	12 years
£1,000,000	13 years

If we can take drug value to be analogous to cheque fraud in Gottfredson *et al.* (1980), with seriousness increasing apace with amount involved, what emerges here, from the highest judicial authority, is an exponent linking seriousness and sentence length which is, as in our experiment, much less than unity.

An interesting study yielding relevant data was that of Sebba (1978). (For recent developments in this work, see Sebba and Nathan, 1984.) His idea was to scale directly the severity of sentence by a magnitude estimation procedure. He simply asked his student subjects to generate numbers corresponding to the severity of different lengths of prison sentence and amounts of fines. Fitzmaurice (1981) undertook some secondary analysis of the Sebba data which seemed relevant. The basis on which it was argued that sentence length can reasonably increase less fast than judgments of offence seriousness is that sentence severity increases faster than sentence length. Fitzmaurice thus plotted sentence length against sentence severity in Sebba's data. More precisely, she plotted log prison sentence length against log sentence severity. Although the fit of the line in reanalysis of Sebba's data is not very good ($R^2 = 0 \cdot 37$), it is interesting that the slope was $0 \cdot 67$. This means that a 67 per cent increase in sentence length is associated with a doubling of sentence severity. Consequently, the assumption that sentence severity would increase faster than sentence length, which is at least consistent with a view of the relationship between offence seriousness and sentence length guessed at earlier, seems justified.

The above reasoning, it should be stressed, was developed from the view that subjects might have been dealing with their task by attempting to ensure a direct one-to-one relationship between offence seriousness and sentence severity rather than sentence length. Adopting such a view, sentence length would be a product of views about both offence seriousness and sentence severity.

An attempt to replicate the finding that sentence severity increased faster than sentence length failed, so this possibility should not be dwelt on. However, the same replication succeeded in showing that offence seriousness did increase at a faster rate than sentence length, the exponent linking the variables being very close to the $0 \cdot 73$ exponent found in the first study described above.

It is worthwhile at this point to mention the decision in *Koyce* ((1979) 1 Cr. App. Rep. (S) 21). Here it was held that 'a sentencer who imposes a series of consecutive terms of imprisonment should review the aggregate ... and reduce it if it appears that the total sentence is excessive, notwithstanding that the individual component sentences are correct and the offences are unrelated'. This is precisely equivalent to saying that, for a set of offences, sentence length should go up at a slower rate than aggregate seriousness. Since Fitzmaurice showed the same thing for single offences, the point is neatly shown from two different sources.

Data on Crown Court judges*

The exclusive use of the ever-available student population was seen by Fitzmaurice (1981) as a possible cause for concern. Also it was recognised that exponents must be calculated for individuals rather than in the aggregate. Consequently Fitzmaurice asked two Crown Court judges whom she met at a seminar on law and psychology to do the same exercise as that done by the students. We will now turn to the results obtained from the Crown Court judges (the inclusion of the third judge in Table 7 will be explained below).

Table 7   *Exponents yielded by three Crown Court judges*

	Judge 1	*Judge 2*	*Judge 3*
SL–Sev	1·00	1·70	–
SL–Ser	0·74	0·45	0·81

Notes
Sev = severity.
Ser = seriousness.
SL = sentence length.

When sentence length was plotted against severity (see Table 7) the first judge was characterised by an exponent of 1 and the other by an exponent of 1·70. The first judge saw an increase in sentence length as associated with an identical proportionate increase in severity. For the second judge, doubling sentence length less than doubles sentence severity. This is particularly interesting for two major reasons. First, we see here two judges exhibiting quite different views about the relationship between sentence length and sentence severity. If retributive justice is concerned with the infliction of a just measure of pain then

---

*Throughout, the phrase 'Crown Court judges' is used as a shorthand reference to judges who sit in the Crown Court, i.e. Circuit judges and High Court judges.

these judges will take different lines in their sentencing even when their retributive sentencing purpose is identical. Second, the conflict of results in the student samples, taken together with the discrepancy between the two judges, at least invites speculation about the role of sentence severity as a mediating variable between seriousness and sentence length.

As far as the relationship between sentence length and seriousness is concerned, the result obtained from real judges is very similar to that obtained from the student sample. The two judges in the first phase of the study, together with a third, are characterised by exponents of $0 \cdot 74$, $0 \cdot 45$ and $0 \cdot 81$. Consequently, the same conclusion can be reached about real judges as we did from the student sample, namely that the exponent is substantially less than one and therefore the doubling of sentence length requires more than a doubling of offence seriousness. What is particularly interesting here is that the judge who saw sentence severity as increasing more slowly than sentence length nonetheless saw sentence length as appropriately increasing slowly in comparison with offence seriousness. This judge obviously sees doubling of offence seriousness as properly leading to a very modest increase in penal pain.

The data reported have consistently shown that the nature of the proportionality link between offence seriousness and sentence length is different from the simplest possible one-to-one increase. However, all the analyses, with the exception of that using Crown Court judges, were on aggregated data. Fitzmaurice (1981) anticipated criticism on this basis. Reanalysing her student data to yield individual exponents, she found a mean exponent of $0 \cdot 59$. However, it should not be thought that Fitzmaurice's work yielded a complete consensus as to the relationship between offence seriousness and appropriate sentence. One further replication yielded exponents in excess of 1, that is sentence length went up faster than offence seriousness. This replication was based on a wider range of offences, and the intriguing possibility exists that the relationship between offence seriousness and appropriate sentence length is itself dependent upon other offence or offender variables. This is not so much damaging to a psychophysical conception of retributive sentencing as indicative of the complexities to be unravelled. The picture is complex rather than random because within the rape study, for example, there was consensus among judges, among students, and between students and judges. Fitzmaurice's research gives us some hope (despite the criticism of Lovegrove (in press) that offence facts rather than offence seriousness should constitute the variables of interest in this sort of analysis) that psychophysics may be applicable to sentencing, and fruitful when applied. Before leaving the Fitzmaurice study, let us speculate in the next section on the significance of the exponent and R^2 measures in the analysis, examine these in relation to the interviews with Crown Court judges undertaken by Fitzmaurice, and finally reach some tentative conclusions.

Indices of sentencing

We see two statistics as central to understanding retributive sentencing. They are the exponent linking judgments of offence seriousness and sentence severity, and the R^2 statistic which indicates the closeness of the relationship between the same variables.

We have analysed the use of the word 'proportionality' in discussions of sentencing. We have found that the simple and direct interpretation of proportionality (that is, a one-to-one increase in the two variables) was not the one which characterised peoples' scaling of the variables against each other. We would suggest that the clarification of the nature of this proportionality is central to a theory of retributive sentencing. In the absence of such clarification, sentence differentials between types of offence, between sentencers, and between individual cases of the same type sentenced by the same judge defy comprehension. Perhaps an analogy would assist the reader to appreciate our fascination with the exponent.

The analogy is with the manufacture of medical thermometers. The thermometer is a device for measuring body temperature which it records in readable form as the extent to which mercury in the instrument expands. In the analogy, the thermometer is the judge who measures culpability (temperature) and records is as the length of time for which an offender is to be deprived of his liberty (mercury expansion). Imagine a factory making thermometers which have a defective scale. The scale is defective in two ways. The first defect is that the scale begins at different points on different thermometers. In a few, the lowest marking is 2mm from the bulb, in a few the lowest marking is 20mm from the bulb, and the remaining thermometers have scales which begin somewhere between these two extremes. This means that a given degree of expansion of the mercury registers different temperatures on different thermometers. The second defect is that the scales themselves are distorted, with the distance between the 95° and 96° markings being less than, equal to, or greater than the distance between 96° and 97° and so on. Thus even for those thermometers whose scales start at the same distance from the bulb, scale distortions may mean that different temperatures will be recorded.

Let us imagine that our thermometer factory has a monopoly. What would be the position of a nurse using the thermometers? If different patients were measured by the same thermometer, you *would* know which patient was hotter. You would not know how much hotter because of the problem with the distorted scale of the instrument. Patients measured by different thermometers could appear to have different temperatures either because they really did have different temperatures or because the thermometer scales were distorted differently or because the scales on the two instruments started at different distances from the bulb. Clearly the usefulness of such thermometers to the nurse would be rather slight. What he would press for would be a change of procedure in the factory so that the scales on each instrument were identical and started at the same distance from the bulb.

In case the precise relationship of the analogy to sentencing is not obvious, let us argue it through. Offenders sentenced by different judges could receive different sentences either because their culpability (temperature) really differed or because of differences in the scale according to which the judges translated offence seriousness into sentence length; either because the scale started at different positions (i.e. for some sentencers an offender had to be more culpable for a custodial sentence to be passed) or because the scales were different (e.g. doubling seriousness more than doubling sentence length for one judge and less than doubling it for another). In other words there are two general types of reason for differences in sentence length. One is difference in the thing to be scaled (the offence) and the other is difference in the characteristics of the scaling instrument (the judge). In current sentencing usage, there is no way of distinguishing between these alternatives.

Before discarding our thermometer analogy completely, let us incorporate the Court of Appeal into it. Sometimes individual readings are corrected by having patients' temperatures checked by readings from one central thermometer revered as accurate for many years. However, only one type of putative error may be referred to the central thermometer, the delay before it takes its reading is immense, the process can be costly, and the central thermometer itself varies, not being effectively bound by its own previous measurements (Pattenden, 1984).

The next question is then 'Why should we want to distinguish between the two potential sources of difference?' The answer is that the second source of difference is, at least in most of its guises, unfair. At present, if two judges sentence the same case, and judge A were to pass a shorter sentence than judge B, it would be impossible to infer from this that judge A thought the offence to be less serious than judge B. Let us suppose that we ask judges to sentence three offences, one of indecent exposure, one of attempted rape, and one of rape. Let us also ask our judges to give, together with their sentence, their estimate of the seriousness of each of the offences. Looking at Table 8 the information which in real life would be available to us from judges sentencing in this way would be sentence lengths (columns headed SL). Looking only at those columns, it could reasonably be

Table 8   *Sentence length and judgments of offence seriousness by three pairs of judges (hypothetical example)*

	Set 1				Set 2				Set 3			
	Judge A		Judge B		Judge C		Judge D		Judge E		Judge F	
	Ser	SL	Ser	SL	Ser	SL	Ser	SL	Ser	SL	Ser	SL
Indecent exposure	100	2	100	2	100	2	100	2	100	2	100	2
Attempted rape	200	4	200	2·8	190	3	225	3	200	4	140	2·8
Rape	300	6	300	3·5	225	4·5	510	4·5	300	6	270	5·4

Notes
Ser = seriousness rating.
SL = sentence length in years.

be assumed that, for example, judge B thought rape and attempted rape less serious than did judge A, and judge F thought them less serious than did judge E. Judge C and judge D passed the same sentence and one might assume that they agreed as to the seriousness of the offences concerned. However, looking at all the information in Table 8 our misconceptions become quite evident.

Judges A and B had made the same seriousness judgments as each other. However, their translation of seriousness score was different. Judge B is characterised by an exponent of 0·5, judge A by an exponent of 1. So while each gave the offences equal seriousness ratings, they differed strikingly in the way they expressed this seriousness in time to be served. As for comparisons between judge C and judge D the same sentences are based upon different views of seriousness. The coincidence of sentence here is a lucky (?) fluke. Considering judge E and judge F, this is the only comparison in which the assumptions are borne out. Judge F gave lower seriousness ratings than judge E and both translated their seriousness scores into sentence length in the same way. Each of the three comparisons made is of interest.

A comparison of the comparisons (!) shows how the end product of a judge's thinking gives no necessary indication as to the relative seriousness of the offences he is considering. The discrepancy, caused by the fact that differences in offence seriousness are not translated in the same way into differences in sentence length, is a function of differing exponents. We would argue that a standard in terms of which to evaluate retributive sentencing should be one in which the same exponent should characterise the relationship between culpability and sentence length for all judges. Attention to this relationship should be given both in initial judicial training and throughout a judicial career. Monitoring judicial performance in these terms on the job rather than during training could be achieved by judges merely giving numerical judgments of seriousness in a random selection of cases. These might then yield an exponent characterising the sentencing function of each individual judge. These would be compared across judges and discussed at judicial seminars. There would be pressure to move towards identical exponents. With identical exponents, differences in sentence length would be unambiguously attributable to differences in judged offence seriousness. Let us be absolutely clear what would be under attack in the procedure suggested. It would not be judges' assessment of individual cases, but the relationship over all cases between their judgments of seriousness and the sentence lengths which they linked with those judgments. If the prescription of that relationship is impossible, or is unacceptable to judges, the possibility of retributive justice does not exist.

The second central index of sentencing was R^2. As the exponent specifies the precise nature of the proportional link between seriousness and penalty, R^2 specifies the degree to which sentencing is retributive. In a retributivist's perfect world, sentence length would be completely predictable from offence seriousness. In the perfect world of someone who believes in individualised justice, sentence should be completely unpredictable from offence seriousness. R^2 specifies the degree of predictability of sentence from offence seriousness. It can vary between 0 and 1. It is quite independent of the exponent, except in that exponents are meaningless with very low R^2. It is simply the square of the product – moment correlation coefficient linking the variables. A judge's performance can be described in terms of, but is not uniquely defined by, knowledge of the two statistics which characterise his performance. A third statistic, the intercept (see Figure 1) is necessary to specify the general level of sentence severity in relation to judgments of offence seriousness. For reasons of presentation and ease of interpretation of the intended use of our model of retributive sentencing, it is excluded from further discussion here. Rather we will attempt to develop a crude classification of judges in terms of the first two statistics. We are confronted by four kinds of judge:

(1) Judges who have low exponents but high R^2 we could refer to as shallow-slope retributivists, since seriousness defines sentence length and sentence length increases slowly relative to seriousness. If the pattern is similar for different types of offence and different types of offender, it is clear that it is the gravity of the offence, not the dangers presented by the person committing it, that is the prime basis for sentence.

(2) Judges who are characterised by a high exponent and a high R^2 could be termed steep-slope retributivists. They are similar to shallow-slope retributivists in that offence gravity 'drives' sentence length, but different from them in that a unit increase in gravity produces a large increase in sentence severity.

(3) Judges who are characterised by a low exponent and a low R^2 could be termed offence-insensitive individualised judges. They are judges who may well conform to a rehabilitation view where seriousness is just one element in sentencing. Therefore lengths of sentence grow slowly as offence seriousness increases. In the limiting case, the exponent would be 0.

(4) Judges with a high exponent but a low R^2 could be termed offence-sensitive individualised judges. Such judges may behave as though deterrence and incapacitation were major sentencing purposes, since, although the extent to which offence seriousness is relevant is limited, in so far as it does operate it increases sentence severity sharply.

The simple classification presented here would be more complex if different offence types generate different statistics. One may illustrate this complexity by asking what the picture would look like given a judge who behaved as though deterrence were only important in the case of violent offending.

A line of argument which could be taken at this point goes as follows: the first four points of the classification system are easy enough to describe. The process becomes more complex when different statistics are linked with different offence types. Is a more complex model worthwhile? Surely judges ought to be able to tell what their sentencing purposes are and how they approach the sentencing task. If judges were able to describe coherently their choice of sentence, and the relationship between sentence length and offence seriousness, the type of analysis described here would become correspondingly less important. We have argued in Chapter 3 that they cannot do this. The next section, describing interviews with Crown Court judges and taken from Fitzmaurice (1981), also bears on the point.

Interviews with Crown Court judges

Lengthy interviews were carried out with the three Crown Court judges who co-operated with the scaling tasks described earlier in this chapter. Two of the judges were interviewed at home, the third in his chambers. The tape-recorded and semi-structured interviews were on average of two hours in length. The three judges went through the scaling exercises and were then left free to speak of their sentencing practice, their use of discretion and their general feeling about the sentencing task. Going through a sentencing exercise took the greater part of the interview for each of the three judges. The judges were asked about the information, if any, they would like to have about the offender or the offence before or during the trial. They were then asked to develop more fully the kind of information they wanted. The role of the interviewer at this point consisted simply in ensuring that the information obtained from the judges was specific and that each of the pieces of information regarded as necessary by the judges was explored fully and in turn. The second part of the sentencing exercise consisted in ascertaining how each of these pieces of information would affect the judge's leniency or harshness in sentencing the offender. The third part of the sentencing exercise consisted in obtaining from each of the judges a scale of sentencing for a hypothetical case following changes in the information regarded as relevant by the judges from information inducing leniency to information inducing greater harshness. It is from the first part of the sentencing exercise and parts of the interviews where judges express freely their feelings about sentencing that the quotations below were extracted.

Looking at sentencing handbooks one could not be optimistic about the level of specificity and clarity being particularly high. Precise analysis of legal arguments contrasts with the more diffuse consideration brought to bear on issues of sentencing. For example Thomas (1979a) writes, 'While in certain contexts the court articulates a principle, or series of principles, in a systematic manner, it is frequently necessary to identify the operative principles from the examination of a considerable number of cases, none of which specifically identify the relevant criteria.'

Given this caveat about the expression of sentencing principles, let us consider the replies of just two of the Crown Court judges. Judge A is characterised by an R^2 of $0 \cdot 77$ and an exponent $0 \cdot 88$. His slope is high (relative to the other judges participating) and he looks like a steep-slope retributivist according to our classification system in comparison with his brother judges and the student subjects. What does judge A say about sentencing practice?

I take the view that whenever there has been a report passed about a man ... it should be brought before the sentencing judge ... I think it is absolutely vital if one is going to pass a sentence which is in the interests of the victim, the public and the man himself ... when a judge passes a sentence, there are so many things which he has got to take into account ... I would like to have the family, and to hear from the wife as to what sort of person he is. I would like to have testimonials from ... employers ... setting out the sort of things he does and whether he is reliable and honest ... Again I suppose this is another aspect of the illogical side of sentencing but one has to consider the effect on the man's family. If he goes to prison ... it is going to break up the family, maybe the children will have to go onto care ... I don't want you to think, when I say that, all a man has to say is 'I have a nice home, I've got a loving wife, this was a one-off thing, please put me on probation, I won't do it again'. It's not as simple as that. It's just in what I call the mental mixer of sentencing ... I think with me probably the fact that the man does have a stable family is something one can build on ... that tells in his favour.

Looking at these statements, one would nearly forget that most of the variance in sentence length was explained by seriousness of offence. In fact, the picture which emerged is one in which the judge claims to take into consideration factors related to the offender even though he emphasises the illogicality of the approach. The idea projected is that of a person who weighs all factors and makes adjustments once everything has gone through the 'mental mixer' to take the future and past of the offender, the offence, the victim and society into account. The story told by the exponent and R^2 is different.

If we turn to the second judge, we can see that he was characterised by an exponent of $0 \cdot 45$ and an R^2 of $0 \cdot 98$. Therefore, one expects someone who is a shallow-slope retributivist. What does this judge tell us about his sentencing practice?

In regard to the present unemployment situation one of the first things I want to know is whether a man is in regular employment or not, because a custodial sentence to a man who is in regular employment is an extremely serious sentence ... One also has to consider the social consequences of sending to prison a man who has got a wife and children because ... you are not only punishing the man, but you are punishing the family ... It is very important in crimes of violence to see whether there are any previous convictions for crimes of violence ... because one of the objects of sentencing people who have committed crimes of violence is to deter them and others ... and if a previous sentence hasn't deterred the crime of violence it may be an indication that the previous sentence was too lenient ... We know that all our prisons are seriously overcrowded. It is a fact of life and we've got to take it into account when considering in every case whether it is necessary ... I don't consider we should add to the overcrowding.

Those are only some of the factors this judge outlined. It attracts the same comment: how could most of the variance be accounted for by the seriousness of the offence when in fact such considerations did not appear to rate highly for this judge in comparison with other factors? At least part of the answer is to be found in the design of the experiment. The offence descriptions perhaps did not include the information which individualised sentencers would have wished to use. Nonetheless the judges did *vary* in R^2. It seems that judges varied in the extent to which they brought other factors, explicit or implied, to bear on the choice of sentence. Thus, although the taxonomy presented earlier will get more complicated, it is still likely to provide a clearer insight into judicial practice than judges' self-report.

We will at this stage deal with some of the criticisms of our approach which we anticipate.

(1) There seems an implicit assumption in the chapter that differences in seriousness ratings between sentencers are fair but that differences in the way in which seriousness ratings are transformed into sentence lengths are not fair. The answer to this is that only if there is a common mode of translating offence seriousness into sentence length are differences in sentencing practice interpretable as differences in perceived seriousness by different judges. Judicial idiosyncrasies then become more evident as such and thereby more capable of modification indirectly through the Court of Appeal or directly in judicial seminars.

(2) There is a stress in the chapter on the exponent measure, but none on the intercept measure. However, the intercept is an extremely important measure, suggesting the offence seriousness appropriate for the shortest prison sentence. We accept this view of the intercept (indeed our thermometer analogy stresses it) but the practical difficulties of its use are such that we did not at this stage wish to discuss it. For the moment, the reader is simply reminded that the exponent will not distinguish between judges characterised by the same proportional relationship between seriousness and sentence length when one is consistently severe and the other consistently lenient (i.e. when they have different intercepts).

(3) It is a common misunderstanding that the value of the exponent depends on the equivalence of offence seriousness scores across judges. Whether or not judge A's offence seriousness score of 50 corresponds with judge B's score of 50 is irrelevant to the use of the exponent. The exponent concerns relations between judgments given by sentencers, not the judgments themselves. Thus, as long as each judge is internally consistent in his estimates, the value of the exponent is unimpaired by differences in judgments of what an offence seriousness score of 50 actually means.

Does proportionality matter?

As a postscript to a chapter on the measurement of proportionality, one must ask oneself whether judges really care about proportionality at any point beyond the pronouncement of sentence. Despite the preeminence of the proportionality principle at the point of sentence there is little evidence that judges concern themselves with proportionality thereafter, at least as far as sentences of imprisonment are concerned. (The situation is different in the United States in so far as mandatory sentencing or sentencing structured by guidelines occurs — see for example Thomas, 1979b.) The evidence for such an assertion derives from, *inter alia*, studies of parole decision-making. The introduction of parole to England and Wales by the 1967 Criminal Justice Act fundamentally changed the effective relationship between time expressed in sentence and time served, yet judicial opposition both at that time and since has been modest in scale and restrained in expression.

To rehearse briefly and partially the parole provisions of the 1967 Act, prisoners became eligible for release on parole licence after one-third of sentence or one year, whichever was the greater. Thus prisoners sentenced to more than eighteen months became eligible for release after one year. Clearly this produces a general 'fuzzing' of the relationship between sentence pronounced and time served such that, for example, a man sentenced to nine years released on licence at the earliest date (after three years) would serve less time than a man sentenced to six years and not released on licence (who will serve four years, given complete remission). One of us, interviewing a senior and distinguished High Court judge for a radio programme nearly a decade ago, posed the question about whether he was troubled by the disproportion which parole introduced. The reply was that he was not troubled by this because the reduction of sentence which parole represented was based on different principles from those which underlie sentence. The obvious supplementary point was put, namely that it was the same sentence which was being changed by the two sets of principles. This cut no ice. As far as the judge was concerned, so long as different principles underpin the decision as to sentence and the decision as to early release, no problems of disproportion exist.

It is worthwhile to cite at some length the comments of Wilkins (1983) on David Thomas's discussion of a case in his book *Principles of Sentencing* (1979a) involving two men with substantial criminal records who admitted to burglaries.

The appellant was sentenced to five years' imprisonment, his co-defendant who was older with 'possibly a worse record' ... was made the subject of a probation order. The Appeal Court upheld the appellant's sentence saying that there was no reason to believe that a variation in his sentence would lead to a change in his behaviour and hence there was no ground for a complaint based on disparity; 'the two disposals were each appropriate along different lines but that does not produce disparity in the true sense of the word.'

Thomas generalises from this position thus: 'in appropriate circumstances, the sentencer may deal with one offender by means of an individualised measure, while following tariff principles for sentencing his co-defendants. As different approaches have been adopted no question of disparity arises.' This seems to say that where the disparity occurs due to disparity between philosophies of sentencing, there is no disparity in the (act of) sentencing! Similarly, in our parole example, the judge held there to be no disparity between sentence passed and sentence served because the principles informing the decision to incarcerate were different from the principles informing the decision to release.

Apart from the general attenuation of the relationship between sentence imposed and sentence served which parole represents, there are certain specific disproportions which were introduced in 1967. The first was that any sentence of between eighteen months and three years had the same earliest date of release. Within that range, the courts were effectively impotent, the actual time served being determined by the paroling authorities. The second specific disproportion introduced by parole flows from the curious fact that time served in prison before sentence did not count towards the twelve-month minimum for parole eligibility but did count towards the one-third minimum. For example, let us take the extreme (but not unrealistic) case of two men who have each served one year in prison before sentence. One is sentenced to eighteen months' imprisonment and the other to six years' imprisonment. They would have become eligible for release on the same day. In this way, the differentials imposed by the courts are reduced by the paroling authorities, and particularly so to the extent to which there has been pre-sentence custody.

The modesty of judicial opposition to the profound changes in the courts' effective powers which occurred because of the introduction of parole may be because there was no real reduction. Executive manipulation of sentence length may be effectively countered by judicial manipulation of sentence length to restore something closer to the *status quo*. If officials decrease proportion of sentence served, judges can respond by increasing the length of sentence pronounced. Fitzgerald and Sim (1979) and Marshall (1974) both assert that something like this happens, and in Marshall's book there is a cartoon of a judge consulting a calculator to make the right adjustments. However, it is quite clear from an examination of average sentence lengths (Walker, 1981) that this has not happened. Crucially, if such adjustments had occurred, a particularly marked reduction in the number of sentences in the eighteen months to three years band would be evident because, as noted earlier, for differentials within this range courts are impotent. No such reduction is evident since parole was introduced. Thus, it seems, once proportionality has informed the act of sentencing, judges seem relatively indifferent to the main-tenance of proportionality in the imposition of sentences. We are tempted to add that this indifference is also inferrable from neglect of differences in impact made by different prison regimes. The prin-ciple that the same sentence should have equal impact across people is negated by differences in prison conditions. A year's sentence served in a local prison is unarguably a worse experience than a year's stay at an open prison. Yet equality of impact according to prison regime receives scant attention, in contrast with the wider application of the principle in calculating fine amounts (see Ashworth, 1983). In short, although the principle of proportionality which underpins this chapter is of real concern and we do not regret our attention to it, it may well be regarded as hollow, because of the lack of concern with proportionality later in the penal process. A research-informed debate about the tenuousness of the relationship between sentence imposed and sentence exacted and judicial attitudes to it would certainly advance our understanding of sentencing psychology.

CHAPTER 7

Preferred numbers, noticeable differences and justice

On 4 February 1884 Sir Edmund du Cane wrote to the Permanent Under-Secretary of State at the Home Office. His opening paragraph would attract the attention of the present incumbent of that post even more surely than that of the incumbent of a hundred years ago. 'Sir', began du Cane, 'I beg leave to request that you will call the attention of the Secretary of State to certain points connected with the terms of the sentences awarded by the various criminal courts, as I venture to think that, if the subject were duly brought under consideration of those who are responsible for the administration of justice, a considerable amount of unnecessary suffering might be saved without any diminution of the efficiency of the law; and that a very appreciable economy in the cost of our penal establishments might be effected.

The 'points' which Sir Edmund had in mind concerned the tendency of courts to make prison sentences of certain lengths rather than others, for example to make sentences of five, seven and ten years rather than six, eight and nine. Part of the problem, Sir Edmnd opined, was derived from judges passing sentences in terms equivalent with periods of transportation conventionally used. He was clearly outraged, arguing that 'It is impossible not to feel that some more exact measurement is possible than is exhibited in the above figures, and, if it is possible, that the present arbitrary practice is incapable of justification.' He pointed to the 'needless suffering' of the prisoner and his family, and to 'the cost of our penal establishments' in suggesting that the more exact measurement he hoped for would result in a net shortening of prison terms. (Du Cane's letter is reproduced in the 1978 Report of the Advisory Council on the Penal System.)

Eleven years later the great Victorian scientist Sir Francis Galton happened upon a summary of prison terms passed. He noted the same pattern as had du Cane, with short sentences clustering around the three-, six-, nine- and twelve-month marks, and longer sentences rounded to years, with even larger gaps between very long sentences which were used. He was fairly acid about this aspect of sentencing:

The extreme irregularity of the frequency of the different terms of imprisonment forces itself on the attention. It is impossible to believe that a judicial system acts fairly which [acts in this way]. Runs of figures like these testify to some powerful cause of disturbance which interferes with the orderly distribution of punishment in conformity with penal deserts.

He continued: 'We may ... be pretty sure that if the year had happened to be divided into 10 periods instead of 12, the exact equivalent of 3 months, which would then have been 2½ [months] would not have been used in its place. If this supposition be correct, the same penal deserts would have been treated differently to what they are now.'

Nearly a century later and, to be frank, in complete ignorance of what had gone before, Margaret Sampson and Ken Pease made the same observation (Pease and Sampson, 1977). In fact the pattern had changed little from that observed by du Cane and Galton. Our first responses to what we found were similar to those of our distinguished predecessors, namely that injustice was involved. We thought in terms of 'just noticeable differences' and reasoned that if a judge thought an offence was just too serious for four years it would be given a sentence, not a four years and one day, not of four years and a quarter, not of four years and a half, but of five years. The extra year would be deemed necessary to make a 'just noticeable difference' to sentence length. We cited an Appeal Court reference to a reduction of sentence from five years to four as 'minimal'. This difference may, we argued, be regarded as minimal from the point of view of the sentencer, but it works out at 243 nights locked up for the prisoner (assuming he is denied parole), and an extra 121 nights assuming he is paroled at the earliest possible date.

This indifference to time within broad bands is taken to be a proper feature of decisions of the Court of Appeal. This is reflected with some acerbity by a judge whose sentences were adjusted:

White and Chalk also appealed against sentence and White's was reduced from 23 to 21 years and Chalk's from 21 to 19. I did not understand the reasons for the reductions. When I was at the Bar, and in my early years as a judge, the Court of Appeal would only interfere with a sentence if it was wrong in principle ... If I may say so, with great respect to the members of that division of the Court of Appeal which considered these appeals, if 21 and 19 years respectively were right, in principle, then 23 and 21 years couldn't

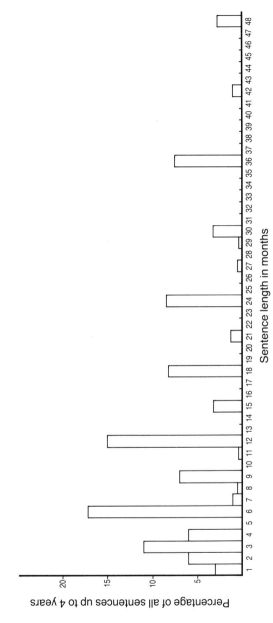

Note Consecutive activated suspended sentences are omitted. The numbers on the abcissa refer to the higher bound of each range.

Figure 2 Frequency of prison sentence by length
Source: from Pease and Sampson, 1977.

have been wrong. With sentence of that duration, two years one way or the other do not affect the principle. (King-Hamilton, 1982)

The notion of the just noticeable difference has a long and reasonably distinguished history. Weber (1846) suggested that the proportion by which a stimulus would have to be changed to become just noticeably different would be a constant proportion of the stimulus; if a 100-gram weight has to be increased by 10 grams to make a just noticeable difference (jnd), a 200-gram weight would have to be increased by 20 grams, a 300-gram weight by 30 grams, and so on. This law, Weber's law, holds reasonably well in the middle ranges of most stimulus dimensions. Given this, the inclination to turn to the just noticeable difference to shed light on patterns of sentence lengths (see Figure 2) was irresistible. Despite this, even brief inspection of Figure 2 shows that no simple proportional increase could generate the sentencing pattern observed, but that there is a perceptible pattern, which will be discussed later. The approach remains attractive, a view in which we are encouraged by recent comments on disparity. Forst (1982) writes:

Operationalising the definition of disparity with absolute time presents ... problems ... Absolute time does not adequately allow consideration of the relative lengths of the sentences imposed. Consider the following cases: a defendant is convicted of robbery and is sentenced to 20 years in prison. A second defendant is convicted of robbery and, with the same degree of culpability and criminal background, receives a sentence of 20 years and six months. A difference of six months, considering the length of the sentences, probably would not shock the consciences of most people. Now compare the sentences of two pickpockets. The first is sentenced to six months in jail, while the second, having committed a similar crime under similar circumstances, receives a sentence of one year. In this situation, the differences between the two sentences is also six months. However a six-month difference here means the second sentence is twice as long as the first. This discrepancy is much more likely to offend people's sense of justice.

If so, this means that 'people's sense of justice' operates on just noticeable differences which are proportions.

The relevance of preferred numbers

An alternative way of looking at the choice of length of sentence would be to take the idea of preferred numbers and assume that the choice of sentence length, expressed in numbers, had to do with some property of the numbers themselves. Indeed, if there were not a marked preference for certain sentence lengths, one would expect that all sentence lengths would be imposed and the gaps in Figure 2 would not have appeared. This important point is worth some expansion. We can envisage the following sentence lengths being given by three different judges:

Judge 1   12, 14, 16, 18 months
Judge 2   13, 15, 17, 19 months,
Judge 3   11, 20, 21, 22 months

When combined, sentences include all lengths (in whole months) from eleven to twenty-two months. In fact, of those twelve sentence lengths, seven were never used by judges.

Baird and Noma (1975) noted that people seemed to prefer certain numbers (twenty-two in all) between 1 and 100 and these twenty-two numbers were the only ones generated by the base numbers (β) 10 and 5 in the function $N = k\beta^n$, where k is an integer between 1 and -1, N is the preferred number and n an integer exponent. Consequently, Fitzmaurice (1981), using the Baird and Noma formulation, generated three tables of numbers using bases 3, 6 and 12. These bases were chosen on the assumption that 3, 6 and 12 would be the appropriate

Table 9   *Preferred sentence lengths (N) in months generated by the bases 3, 6 and 12 (using Baird and Noma's function $N = k\beta^n$)*

$k\backslash\beta^n$	3^0	3^1	3^2	3^2	6^0	6^1	6^2	12^0	12^1
1	1	3	9	27	1	6	36	1	12
2	2	6	18	–	2	12	(72)	2	(24)
3	–	–	–	–	3	18	(108)	3	36
4	–	–	–	–	4	24	(144)	4	48
5	–	–	–	–	5	30	(180)	5	(60)
6	–	–	–	–	–	–	–	6	(72)
7	–	–	–	–	–	–	–	7	(84)
8	–	–	–	–	–	–	–	8	(96)
9	–	–	–	–	–	–	–	9	(108)
10	–	–	–	–	–	–	–	10	(120)
11	–	–	–	–	–	–	–	11	(132)

Note
Numbers in brackets indicate predictions of preferred sentence lengths beyond the 48-months limit of the Pease and Sampson (1977) data.

ones, when years or parts of years are involved. The numbers generated appear as Table 9. So, for example, the number in the top left hand corner of the matrix is the result (N) of the sum $N = k\beta^n$, where k is 1, β is 3 and n i 0. Table 9 contains the results of all similar sums in the range covered by Pease and Sampson (1977). To restate the purpose of this exercise, it is to demonstrate an (attempted) rule for number preference which generates all the sentence lengths which judges use and none of those which they do not use. What the table shows is that the correspondence between sentence lengths predicted and used is only moderate. Inspection of Table 9 alongside Figure 2 will show that some sentences are predicted which are not used and some are used which are not predicted.

The re-emergence of the jnd?

It is interesting that in Table 9 the different base numbers (β) look better for different ranges of sentence length. The base number 6 is least unimpressive in the range twelve to thirty-six months, and the base 12 best corresponds to intuitions about sentence length over thirty-six months. Fitzmaurice (1981) speculated that there may be a simple rule of number preference operating, namely that people use numbers with bases of 3, 6 and 12 and change the base as sentence length increases. So, for example, one would operate with multiples of 3 with short sentences, with multiples of 6 with middle-range sentences and on a scale based on 12 for long sentences. In Figure 3 the reader will see lines joining the tops of those columns of the histogram which would be sentences given according to each scale but not the next longer one, that is the three-month scale as unit points of 3, 9, 15, etc., and the six-month scale as points of 6, 18 and 30 which only it predicts. The twelve-month scale does not have any points which only it predicts, but it is clear that there are many more sentences of say twenty-four months than would be expected from the use of three- and six-month scales alone. On Figure 3 (line (a) shows sentences based on three months, (b) on six months and (c) on twelve months. It seems from Figure 3 that judges do appear to use three overlapping distributions based on three, six and twelve months.

Earlier it was mentioned that the issues of preferred sentence lengths had been discussed a century before Pease and Sampson. Figure 4 shows such a distribution transformed from population figures (see Pease, 1980) given in Appendix D of the Report of the

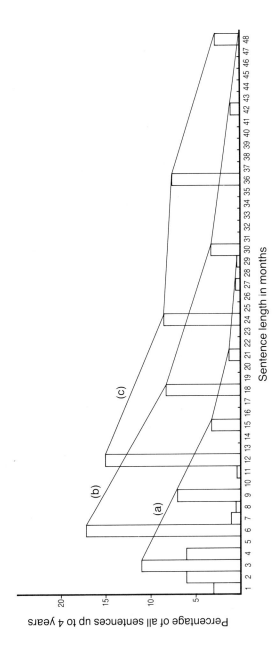

Note Consecutive activated suspended sentences are omitted. The numbers on the abcissa refer to the higher bound of each range.

Figure 3 Frequency of prison sentence by length: overlapping scales
Source: from Pease and Sampson, 1977

Advisory Council on the Penal System (1978). Figure 4 makes it evident that five years is the sentence length whose multiples constitute preferred numbers in this range with a subsidiary preference based on seven years (no doubt because of the relevance of the seven-year period to conversion from sentences of transportation (see Thomas, 1978a, b)).

The question remains as to why the preferred scale changes. Why is it that three-month units apply to shortish sentences, six and twelve months for longer ones and five years for very long ones? The change in scales itself cannot be explained in terms of preferred numbers. Strangely enough it is the notion of the jnd which lends itself to an explanation of scale change. Past thirty months, offences must be too serious to be scaled in modest three-month increments and so attract six-month increases. In the same way the six-month scale is gradually replaced by a twelve-month scale. The situation with very short sentences is not as clear as would be inferred from the section above. It seems reasonable to assume that for very short sentences a scale based on one or two months is necessary. However, the overlapping distributions are interesting. Why is it that the use of the three-month scale end completely at thirty months? Why does the six-month scale end at forty-two months (probably)? If one works out the ratio of the increase involved in moving between adjacent used sentence lengths of one year or more, increases in sentence length vary between 10 and 25 per cent. This is a relatively narrow range, certainly much narrower than would be the case if any of the scales were to be used throughout the sentencing range, or if the scales did not overlap.

Preliminary conclusions on the choice of sentence length

A tentative account of the process underlying choice of sentence length may now be hazarded. It is consistent with the preceding analysis of sentencing patterns but is in the nature of a hypothesis rather than a unique inference from sentencing practice.

When a sentencer judges an offence to merit a sentence of imprisonment of, let us say, between six and eighteen months, he will provisionally light upon a figure within that range which is a multiple of three months – either six, nine, twelve, fifteen or eighteen months. If he is thinking in the range eighteen months to three years, he will choose a sentence length which is a multiple of six months, i.e. eighteen, twenty-four, thirty or thirty-six months. If he is thinking

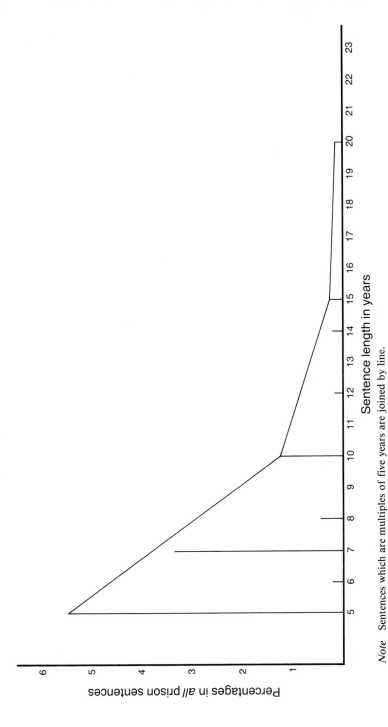

Note Sentences which are multiples of five years are joined by line.

Figure 4 Sentence length by percentage of sentences passed (1883 data)

in the range three to six years (?) he may well think first of a sentence length which is a multiple of twelve months, i.e. thirty-six, forty-eight, sixty or seventy-two months. Having made his tentative choice he will consider factors in mitigation or aggravation on the basis of which to adjust sentence length. Let us take the eighteen-months to three-year range as an example, with a provisional choice of a sentence of thirty months. We think it likely that a degree of mitigation would reduce sentence by six months in such a case to two years. A reduction of three months is possible but such a reduction verges on the imperceptible. The reduction of 12 months would represent too great a proportion. The reduction of sentence by mitigation is a convenient way of making the point that proportional reduction of sentence length would need to be within the narrow band (10 to 25 per cent) to be acceptable.

One may argue that the same principle applies in sentencing generally. An interesting piece of evidence consistent with this view comes from a totally unexpected quarter, the 1977 Report of the Advisory Council on the Penal System, *The Length of Prison Sentences*. There we read: 'at this juncture we wish merely to pose a few simple questions. Are there not cases of two years' imprisonment where 18 months, or 15 or even less, might safely be passed?' It will be noted that the sentence below two years is conceived as eighteen months (a gap of six months) and the sentence below that fifteen months (a gap of three months) just as would be predicted by the hypothesis set out. Recall too the Court of Appeal's view cited earlier that a 20 per cent reduction of sentence from five years was 'minimal'. By this analysis, the roughly 10 per cent reduction to which Judge King-Hamilton objected verges on the imperceptible.

In summary, sentencing scales based on the few preferred numbers used so that no sentences are more than 25 per cent or less than 10 per cent higher than the sentence below would yield predictions roughly in line with current sentencing practice. It seems, therefore, that the rejection of the jnd may well have been premature and that Weber's constant (or in this case limited range) is relevant. The linked phenomena of number preference and jnd scaling of sentences cannot be unimportant. Ashworth (1983) believes that 'the fact that the lengths of sentence are largely conventional may give some grounds for optimism about the possibility of change', although, as Wilkins (1983) notes, 'where these patterns appear they have been extremely persistent over time'. Both du Cane and Galton, especially Galton, saw injustice in this pattern of sentencing, because sentence length does not reflect 'penal deserts'. Pease and Sampson (1977) also believed that the pattern revealed injustice.

We believe they were all wrong, essentially because the evidence of the last chapter appears to indicate that judgments of offence seriousness increased faster than the sentence length to which an offender was assigned. Thus the long-sentence prisoner is not given a sentence disproportionate to the gravity of his offence. What the pattern of preferred numbers and jnds shows is rough justice, not injustice. Judges increase sentence length apace with what they regard as culpability. They are approximate in their sentence lengths because they are approximate in their assessment of culpability: in this sense the crudity of assignation of sentence lengths does not seriously distort the proportionality between culpability and sentence length. Nonetheless, there are important implications of the work for penal policy. First, number preferences in sentencing should be taken into account in framing legislation. Second, the use of conventional number preferences in sentencing choice probably protects sentencers from thinking about what a sentence means in practice, and the implications of this need to be explored.

Tactical legislation

Sentencers use numbers in particular ways. This fact can be used, subtly, in legislation, as is clearly already recognised in some quarters. Sentences of imprisonment conventionally take the form of multiples of three, six and twelve months. Fines typically are expressed as multiples of £5 or £10. Sentencing to imprisonment is duodecimal, sentencing to fines is decimal. When one wants to introduce a sentence which the courts will use instead of imprisonment, what should its substance be expressed in multiples of? Clearly, three, six and twelve. It was cunning of those who introduced community service orders to consider 120, and finally accept 240 hours as the maximum number of hours which may be ordered, since the upper end of community service thereby has associations with sentencing to imprisonment, which it would not have had if, say, 250 hours had been the maximum. There is a counter-intuitive prediction here which would be worth testing, namely that the offences and/or records of people sentenced to numbers of hours divisible by twelve (e.g. 180) are worse than those given slightly longer orders not so divisible (e.g. 200). One hopes that this relatively simple study could be carried out. In any event, analysis of 441 orders from a probation area in the North-east of England showed a significantly higher proportion of long orders whose hours were divisible by six than of short orders. On the basis that longer orders are more likely to have been an alternative to imprisonment, it may be that this shows indirectly the links between duodecimal preference and sentencing to imprisonment.

The duodecimal pitching of community service was exceptional. Typically the thresholds for innovations like suspended sentences, youth custody and parole have periods set as their boundaries which are six months or multiples of six months. Let us take parole as an example of how tactical legislation based on number preference might have helped. Parole eligibility was set at twelve months or one-third of sentence, whichever is the longer. Thus those sentenced to eighteen months' imprisonment were not eligible for parole. Eighteen months is a very popular sentence length (among sentencers; it is less popular among those sentenced). If people sentenced to eighteen months could have been paroled, even with only a short licence period, a significant decrease in prison population could have been achieved. For example, if parole eligibility had been set at ten months or one-third of sentence, back-of-an-envelope calculations suggest that the prison population could have been reduced by perhaps 300 on the basis of earlier release of those sentenced to eighteen months alone. Obviously earlier release of longer-sentence prisoners would increase this figure substantially. Similarly, substantial savings would be made under the early release scheme just introduced at the time of writing if the threshold were to be set at five months instead of the suggested six. Savings could also be made by setting the youth custody threshold at six months and one day rather than four months and one day. The use of detention centres for six-month sentences, with their greater rate of remission, would reduce the use of custody overall. Quite simply and generally, we are suggesting that legislators look at conventional time-fixing in sentencing and set thresholds accordingly.

Doing time and marking time

In their article of that title, Margaret Sampson and Ken Pease suggested that the very use of conventional units of time by sentencers made it easy for them to forget the meaning of the sentence for the prisoner. Three months is quick in the saying but long in the living.

We have already argued that the use of conventional time units means rough justice, not injustice. It is not inconsistent with that to say that fuller recognition of the experience of time passing for the prisoner could lead to a general reduction in sentence lengths. Sampson and Pease thought that one way of doing this was by means of expressing sentence in unconventional units. A small experiment by them (with people who were not judges) showed that when sentences were expressed in units of weeks, sentences imposed were spectacularly shorter than sentences passed on the same cases in year units. Other ways of bringing home to the judge the reality for the prisoner of the sentence imposed might include reference to life events: 'You will serve two years. Since you have a wife and three children, you will miss ten family birthdays, two Christmases, New Years and Easters, forty-two home games at Old Trafford ...'; or to death: 'You will serve two years. Since you are 50, and can expect to live until you are 70, that means you will spend 10 per cent of your remaining life in prison.' Bringing home to the sentencer the extent of what he is inflicting, from which reality he is in part protected by the use of conventional time units in sentencing, is bound to change sentencing practice, probably dramatically.

CHAPTER 8

Responsibility, mitigation and aggravation

The concept of responsibility is central to the sentencing process. It is so primarily because the idea of punishment rests on it. A judge could not pass sentence if there were no responsibility implied or imposed. Even offences of strict liability or offences where the offender is considered irresponsible for his actions take a position in relation to the concept of responsibility.

However, one could argue that responsibility need not be discussed here since the finding of guilt, which constitutes the formal assessment or admission of responsibility, precedes the sentencing stage. This would be an easy way to deal with the question. But the question does emerge in many guises throughout the sentencing process. One example is that of the relation between offence seriousness and offender's culpability. Despite the evidence from Reidel (1975) and Walker (1978) that varying offender description did not change judgments of offence seriousness, attribution theories lead us to think that the relationship between offence, victim, offender characteristics, and culpability may well prove intricate. Another example is that of sentencing following pleas in mitigation. Mitigation (or aggravation) necessarily incorporates an assessment of responsibility. A last example is that of judges' reasons for sentence. The way in which such reasons are worded often implies that an assessment of moral responsibility has been made and is relied upon to warrant particular sentences. The assertion by Devlin (1979) that the degree of moral guilt is regarded as an important determinant to the severity of the sentence makes it even more compelling for us to look at the meanings of this concept, at the way assessments of responsibility are carried out and finally to raise questions about the role of responsibility given its philosophical ramifications in terms of freedom and punishment.

The first problems encountered concern the meaning of responsibility and its relation to the various words covering this concept in one way or another: culpability, liability, causality, blameworthiness, accountability, morality, etc. When, for example, Rawls (1971) states: 'For if, say, statutes are not clear in what they enjoin and forbid, the citizen does not know how he is to behave', and later 'But if the precept of no crime without a law is violated, say by statutes being vague and imprecise, what we are at liberty to do is likewise vague and imprecise', his emphasis is clearly on a legislative construction of responsibility. You can only be held responsible for a breach of particular legal norms. This form of responsibility can only be equivalent to a moral judgment if we assume that the laws coincide with morality. In this sense legal responsibility is culpability. However, does the idea of responsibility also require that there be established a causal link between behaviour and effect? Is liability synonymous with responsibility? In his classification of differing meanings of the term 'responsibility' Hart (1968) distinguishes role, causal, liability and capacity responsibilities and stresses that 'the statement that a man is responsible for his actions or for some act or some harm, is usually not identical in meaning with the statement that he is liable to be punished or to be made to pay compensation for the act or the harm'.

The questions raised by any attempt to differentiate between responsibility and liability for punishment are located at two levels. The first concerns the underlying link between responsibility and punishment, namely free will — one could conceivably be liable for punishment without an assumption of free will but cannot be deemed responsible without an assumed freedom to choose how to act. However, because punishment is made contingent upon free will via the idea of responsibility, the latter becomes equivalent — at times — with liability for punishment. The second level concerns the treated links between responsibility and liability. For example, Hart argues that defining criminal responsibility entails assessing the behaviour in terms of 'criteria' of responsibility.

The complications so far as sentencing is concerned are certainly due to an intertwining in these semantic and conceptual riddles: confusion reigns about what kind of responsibility is assessed, when it is assessed, how the task is performed and whether one kind of responsibility ascription has an effect on the assessment of other forms of responsibilities.

The first point raised concerns free will and responsibility; the latter implies the former — or, put differently, the concept of responsibility denies the existence of determined behaviour. (It is interesting to note in this respect Hart's answer to criticism that man cannot be responsible for his own actions as a man does not produce or cause his own actions. Hart replies: 'But this argument would prove far too much. It would rule out as improper not only the expression ''responsible for his actions'', but also our saying that a man was responsible vicariously or otherwise for harmful outcomes which he had not caused, which is a perfectly well established legal usage'!) The ability to choose to perform or to omit to do something is a prerequisite to an assessment of responsibility. Rawls puts it so: 'The essential point here is that principles that best conform to our nature as free and equal rational beings themselves establish our accountability.'

However, considerable doubts have been placed on the notion of free will in the psychological literature. Many personality theories, for example, are underlined by a deterministic view of man even if the reasons for proposing this determinism varies. For example, Hjelle and Ziegler (1981) affirm that:

deterministically based personality theories differ markedly on the nature of these factors. For example, human behaviour could be determined by uncon- scious motives, external reinforcements, early experiences, physiological processes, cultural influences – each one open to various interpretations. The major source of agreement among these types of personality theories, in this context, is that human behaviour is determined.

Freud's psychodynamic theory offers a deterministic view of man through its emphasis on the unconscious, but Skinner (1971) is probably the psychological theorist whom one would link most closely with the demise of freedom. For him 'autonomous man is a device used to explain what we cannot explain in any other way. He has been constructed from our ignorance and as our understanding increases, the very stuff of which he is composed vanishes.'

In fact Skinner's position, as bold as it may still appear despite the number of years which have elapsed since its original formulation, rejects the traditional concept of responsibility and consequently punishment. Since he sees the natural and social environments as determining behaviour, he argues that it is by changing their attributes that behaviour will be changed:

The real issue is the effectiveness of techniques of control. We shall not solve the problems of alcoholism and juvenile delinquency by increasing a sense of responsibility. It is the environment which is 'responsible' for the objectional behaviour, and it is the environments, not some attribute of the individual, which must be changed. (Skinner, 1971)

He also makes a point concerning responsibility which is also pertinent to the argument in Chapter 1 about the powerful:

The literature of freedom and dignity have made the control of human behaviour a punishable offence, largely by holding the controller responsible for aversive results. The controller can escape responsibility if he can maintain the position that the individual himself is in control. The teacher who gives the student credit for learning can also blame him for not learning. The parent who gives his child credit for his achievements can also blame him for his mistakes. Neither the teacher nor the parent can be held responsible.

The same reasoning could equally well apply to judges personally or to the society judges represent. Some offenders are blamed and punished, and society is exonerated of responsibility. This reasoning has started to show signs of fatigue. For example, Pease (1979) in relation to crime prevention, showed that refusal by the Danish authorities to prosecute for theft of less than 500 kr from shops has led to a diminution of such incidents because this policy incites shops to take better preventive measures. A refusal to act on the basis of the individual responsibility of thieves has led to changes in the environment which themselves have controlled the occurrence of future thefts. Society did not have to locate responsibility at the level of the individual nor did it have to resort to the punishment of individuals, or to sustain high social costs of processing thieves through the penal process.

Even if Skinner's view is abrasive and alien to many, it raises a number of issues which are centrally relevant to the concept of responsibility. However, we have suggested that, for judges, the ascription of responsibility, whatever the reality, is important in sentencing. The question is then to know what happens under a system which wholeheartedly embraces the notion of freedom, in terms of both the ascription of and exoneration from responsibility.

In his excellent article 'On Mental Elements and Their Place in Psychology and Law' (1981), Derek Blackman states the problems as follows:

The criminal law in the United Kingdom is of course constantly confronted by this very issue in judging whether an accused person is providing an adequate and truthful explanation of his conduct. 'An act does not make a man guilty of a crime unless his mind be also guilty' and so criminal law, though designed to influence what we do rather than what we think, is permeated by the need to interpret or attribute mental elements to which the accused person alone has direct access and which can therefore only be inferred by others from what he says or from the circumstances of the crime.

Hart's classification referred to earlier included in its dual meaning of imputability and of fault as one criterion by which to assess criminal responsibility. Derek Blackman expounds in his article the radical behaviourist position in relation to the use of private mental events in criminal proceedings. Two of the points raised by him are particularly relevant to our discussion of responsibility. Blackman states: '"Behaviourists" analysis of the language of private enterprise emphasizes (as do other analyses) that words or concepts may become diffuse when detached from potential external referents.' The implications of the radical behaviourist approach suggest that judges should not only provide verbal statements but give us elements of assessment by reference to the circumstances: namely that judges should name explicit the way in which their appreciation of the specific features of the case led them to pass a specific sentence (or reduce it because of mitigation). Blackman points out that 'courts of law have been prepared, to a greater or lesser extent, to evaluate whether a required mental element in crime existed by reference to the circumstances *in addition* to the self-report of the accused person'. If behaviourists would agree that such evidence is crucial, they would not restrict it to the assessment of *mens rea* in the offender but would see it as a general operating principle. It becomes equally applicable to judges in the sense that reasons for sentence (self-report) should also be complemented by information on the circumstances pertaining to the sentence. (See the discussion on reasons for sentence in Chapter 3.)

Let us turn now to Blackman's second point. The passage is long but is worth quoting in full:

Skinner has argued within his deterministic and environmental analysis that we give a person credit for his achievements to the extent that we can see no other explanation for his behaviour (Skinner 1971) ... The argument can be extended to the concept of blame. Perhaps we tend to blame a person for his conduct in relation to our inability to identify any influences on his behaviour ... A failure to identify such extenuating circumstances leads to a tendency to attribute the behaviour to 'internal' cognitive events ...

However behaviourist analysis of cognitive events in normal people emphasises that they can be seen as dependent variables. This view, of course, raises questions about whether it is appropriate to blame a person or hold him legally responsible for his actions *because* of any reported (or inferred) cognitive events.

The problems linked to verbal reports of internal mental processes evoked in Chapter 3 emerge again in relation to ascription of responsibility. Another interesting question raised by Blackman in this passage concerns the attribution of motives in the absence of observed or stated environmental influences (see Chapter 3). An area of psychology deals precisely with attribution generally and attribution of responsibility more specifically. It is to this literature that we will turn now.

We owe much to the analysis of Shaver (1975) and the argument presented here follows his closely. Attribution theory recognises three meanings of responsibility: causality, legal accountability and moral accountability. Shaver argues that attribution theorists use the term responsibility in its last sense. It is arguable that judges when sentencing an offender use it also in this sense and not solely as legal accountability. Shaver points out that 'exaggerations of causality and legal accountability' may arise because of particular motivation and that 'beliefs in moral culpability or laudability ... can serve personal needs to such a degree that objective reality may never sway them'.

Shaver defines three causes for the attribution of varying degrees of responsibility. Personality differences may affect the ascription. For example individuals having a strong internal locus of control (i.e. people who tend to see themselves as largely in control of events in their lives) will operate as though others have equally high internal loci of control. In other words 'we generalise from our own circumstances, assuming that other people have about the same degree of control over their lives as we feel we have over our own'. In a similar vein, it is arguable and consistent with doubts expressed by Blackman on blame and by radical behaviourists on responsibility that a judge's belief in free will and choice will lead to harsher judgments of responsibility (although not necessarily to harsher sentences (see Chapter 3).

Dogmatism can also lead to differing judgments of responsibility and in the same way. Shaver argues that 'we would expect highly dogmatic people to be less aware of extenuating circumstances' and that perception of the whole event by then will become distorted, emphasising the behaviour of the actor as sole explanation for the event, to the detriment of other contributory variables such as circumstances.

Another factor Shaver deals with is that of distortions in the motivation of the assessor. The work cited in this respect is of direct relevance and also of intrinsic interest. He argues that one such distortion concerns what Lerner (1970) calls the 'belief in a just world'. If individuals believe that the world is a just place then the outcomes befalling other people must be deserved either because of what they did or because of their moral responsibility. An experiment by Lerner and Matthews (1967) shows nicely the relationship established between behaviour and moral accountability in relation to suffering. In brief, the experiment led to the following results: people rated as unattractive other people for whose suffering they believed they were responsible. However, when people did not believe they were responsible for the suffering of the other, the rating of the suffering person was positive. Shaver argues that a 'perceiver's need to believe in a just world may distort his evaluations of an innocent victim. When an attribution of responsibility ... is made impossible by the situation, an attribution of moral accountability will be made in order to justify suffering.' In other words, an offender may be perceived as meriting a particular sentence solely on the ground that he is a bad person. This presumably is the kind of reasoning which may underpin sentencing of offences committed under the influence of alcohol, or to feed a drug habit. It may be helpful for the reader to keep the issue in mind during the discussion of mitigation later in the chapter.

Shaver proposes that 'defensive attribution' may govern the ascription of responsibility. In this process, the assessment of responsibility can be constrained by two factors. The first is situational possibility. If a judge believes it possible that he himself could be placed in a similar situation to that of the defendant he has no other choice than to attribute responsibility to the defendent so as to preserve his image of himself as 'not a criminal'. On the other hand if 'personal similarity' is implied – that is, if the judge believes that he is similar to the person whose behaviour he is assessing – chance is more likely to be invoked as explanation of the offence.

A tentative formulation of responsibility assessment on the basis of the work of both Lerner and Shaver seems appropriate to the situation which confronts the judiciary. First of all, a judgment in terms of causality is tried: is the case straightforward, with the offender *causing* the offence event to occur? If the answer is yes, there is no *need* to infer moral responsibility as a rationale for sentence (although the act may be judged immoral). If the answer is negative, judges have to decide if the situation is one in which they could possibly find themselves (situational possibility) or if they perceive personal similarity with the accused. If the former is chosen, they assert responsibility (keeping in mind that they then perceive the actor as behaving in ways they personally would not have done); if the latter applies, chance is invoked and assessment of responsibility diminished or set equal to naught. Finally, if neither situational possibility nor personal similarity applies, a sentence is passed and moral responsibility inferred from it. Figure 5 summarises this decision-making process graphically. In this tentative description of the decision process regarding responsibility one thing is striking: moralistic reasons could only be a clue to a non-causal case but would hide the difference between assessing responsibility prior to sentence and inferring it from the sentence.

Two main points have been made so far in this chapter. The first is that regardless of the kind of responsibility involved, it is evident that psychological mechanisms are at play in determining its assessment. Radical behaviourism and attribution theories provide some insights into the important and complex decision-making process in which judges are involved.

The second point on which we now want to elaborate stresses that the concept of responsibility is centrally relevant to sentencing practice. It is relevant because without the idea of responsibility, and consequently of free will and choice, there could not exist a sentencing system as we know it. A sentence is a statement of responsibility mediated by the provisions of law. It would be folly to think that, once the question of guilt has been settled, responsibility can be dismissed. Judgments about sentence length need not involve *a priori* judgment of moral responsibility (and in some cases, civil mainly, it does not) but judicial practice has it as such. Lord Devlin (1979) emphasises this point beyond any reasonable doubt! Considering the contention that 'the offender's moral guilt is not a matter with which the law is concerned', he states:

This is not how in fact the law is administered. The degree of moral guilt is not the only determinant of the severity of the sentence but it is universally regarded as an important one. It manifests itself in two ways. Firstly, in the gradation of offences in the criminal calendar: in order of gravity they are not arranged simply according to the harm done. Secondly, by taking into

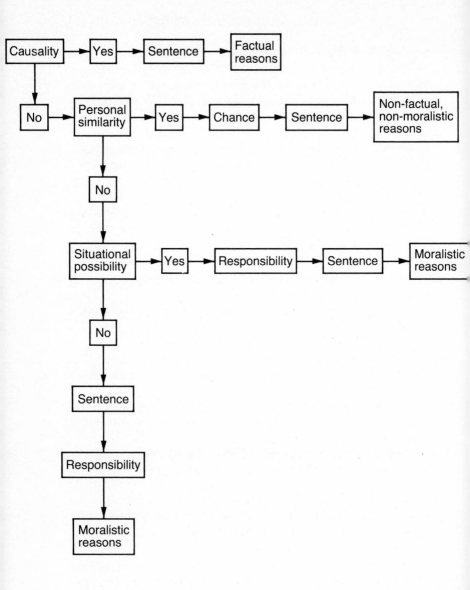

Figure 5 Sentencing and the attribution of responsibility

account the wickedness in the way the crime is committed: sentences for theft are not graded simply according to the amount stolen nor even according to more refined methods of estimating the harm done.

But the infiltration of moral norms in the sentencing process under the guise of moral responsibility does not stop there and the puzzle in fact grows in difficulty when Devlin (1965) argues that 'a judge may proportion his sentence according to the degree of immorality involved in the act itself but not according to extraneous immorality'! What else is mitigation or aggravation if not a process through which moral responsibility and hence morality lead to the apportionment of a sentence on the basis of sometimes very extraneous morality/ immorality. How else would anyone be able to explain sentence reduction on the basis that the offender had, at a point in time unrelated to the crime, saved the life of a child (see Ashworth, 1983)? Judgments about, for example, how much of a sentence should be discarded because of the victim's behaviour or the offender's employment record (see Wilkins, 1983) amounts to asking the question: how much less responsible is this offender, given that the victim did this or iven that the offender has always been trustworthy with regard to is employer? Mitigation or aggravation entail by necessity a re-estimation of the liability to be punished through a consideration of factors which are concerned with a more global assessment of the 'morality' of the accused (and his victim notoriously so in cases of rape). Finally, do judgments about the responsibility of the offender mean judgments in relation to what was actually done (responsibility for the act) or what was intended? *Mens rea* is an essential part of the assessment of responsibility and within this context a judgment on the state of mind of the accused is required. We have reflected on the difficulties inherent in such a task earlier in this chapter, but another facet of such a task involves assessing what the accused actually intended to do. Is the concept of a guilty mind restricted to what the accused actually did (i.e. break the particular legal rule for which he is prosecuted)? A man may intend to commit a robbery but because of the environment at the time only commit burglary for which he is prosecuted. On the other hand an unpremeditated theft may lead to a charge of theft and assault if the circumstances lend themselves to it. What are judges really assessing when they sentence: the degree of responsibility given that the state of mind of the accused was such that he intended committing a more or less serious offence? If as we have seen moral assessment is an integral part of the process, would the first case be judged more severely? Would this also decrease the severity in the second case?

Mitigation and aggravation

The right to inflict punishment does not flow directly from the characterisation of an event as harmful. The raw material of the culpability judgment is the act (or occasionally the failure to act). The process of assigning culpability 'becomes activated when an authorised individual recognises an event as a serious harm to a person or property' (Wilkins, 1983). Three other sets of information beside the act are identified by Wilkins as being relevant to the determination of culpability, namely the actor, the acted upon and the environment in which the act takes place. At the point of conviction, all the information which the court will have available about the act, the victim and the context has been made available. A process is then initiated in which the sentencer considers aspects of the actor which will eventuate in a sentence. This sentence may be different from that which would have been passed in the absence of any additional information about the offender.

A circumscription of the topic of this part of the chapter to events between conviction and sentence is a shameless attempt to avoid difficulties in distinguishing between factors impacting on judgments of offence gravity and those impacting on judgments of culpability. Despite the evidence from Reidel (1975) and Walker (1978) that varying offender description did not change judgments of offence seriousness, it remains intuitively appealing to believe that major changes in the perception of the offender will change the image of the act, as it is appealing to believe that changes in the image of what happened will change inferences made about a person who is accused on such an act. Thus, for example, awareness of a long series of violent sexual offences in an accused's record may well increase the imagined brutality and extent of harm caused in a violent sexual offence under consideration. If this is correct, there is an indissoluble link between judgments of seriousness and judgments of culpability. However, by concentrating on considerations of court process one may partly avoid the difficulties introduced by this relationship and grappled with earlier in this chapter. This will only be partial because, as will be seen, one mitigation tactic is to represent the offence as less serious than it may appear to be (and hence the actor as less culpable). The facts of the case presented may be particularly meagre where there is a guilty plea. Shapland (1981) shows clearly that a much higher number of mitigating factors connected with the offence itself occur after a plea of guilty, because the defence has had no earlier opportunity of informing the court of the defendant's account of events.

The difficult relationship between offence seriousness and offender characteristics was glossed over in Chapter 6 where culpability and seriousness were used almost interchangeably. Their separation has implications for the meaning of the R^2 statistic but is not crucially damaging to its use in the ways suggested in that chapter.

Perhaps the first thing to note about mitigation and aggravation in sentencing is that they do not have equal status as sentencing principles. Mitigation is much more prominent in the literature than aggravation and is accorded formal status in the court, where the defence has the right to make a plea in mitigation while the prosecution has no equivalent right to make a plea in aggravation. In Thomas's authoritative (1979a) *Principles of Sentencing*, there is a whole chapter on mitigation yet aggravation does not even appear in the index. Thomas's summary of his reading of the principles of sentencing from Court of Appeal decisions suggests why this is so. He argues that:

the process of calculating the length of a tariff sentence involves three stages − defining a scale of sentences in relation to the most typical instances within the general category of the offence concerned, fixing by reference to that scale the level of sentence which would be appropriate to the facts of the particular offence committed by the offender and finally, making such allowances for mitigating factors as may be just by reducing the sentence below that level.

It would be much more difficult to justify increasing sentence by reference to facts about the offender, although the limits of Court of Appeal influence are evident in King Hamilton's (1982) account of his sentencing practice:

My method of approach to this problem is, first, to assess the sentence appropriate to the offence. I then consider if it should be adjusted *upwards* in the light of the previous criminal record (if any). Next, it has to be adjusted downwards, by giving credit for having pleaded guilty (and not having gone into the witness box and lied). I then take into consideration any valid points made in counsel's speech in mitigation of sentence. (emphasis added)

What seems like mercy when one sentences less severely than an offence merits looks like malice when one sentences more severely. This is one of the reasons, no doubt, why debates about sentencing the dangerous offender tend to be so acrimonious. The stated position of the Court of Appeal may or may not accord with a review of its practice, still less the practice of lower courts. However, the position that there is no aggravation–mitigation continuum is at least tenable psychologically. There are good examples in psychology of contexts in which different factors are involved in what seems at first blush to be a continuum. For example Herzberg *et al.* (1957) showed that it was less realistic to think in terms of a continuum of satisfaction with work to dissatisfaction with work constructed from the same set of factors. They showed it to be more realistic to think in terms of two types of factor, motivators and hygiene factors, operating in different ways. Hygiene factors are those which determined whether a worker was dissatisfied or not, motivators were those which determined whether satisfied or not. For example working conditions could help to eliminate dissatisfaction, but could not generate satisfaction. Responsibility offered to the employee was much more relevant to the generation of satisfaction than to the elimination of dissatisfaction. In the same way, different factors may influence aggravation and mitigation.

One possibility is that aggravation operates on features of the act and mitigation on characteristics of the actor. In the light of this speculation it is interesting to note some recent findings of Wilkins (1983). He writes: 'A study of court reports and other sources enabled a provisional list of factors said to be of either aggravation or mitigation to be compiled. The list was then presented to persons in the field and their views on additional items were solicited. A total of 40 items were obtained by these methods – 20 aggravating and 20 mitigating.' The two lists are reproduced as Table 10.

The position from which Wilkins was working was one where aggravating factors could increase sentence length. Specifically, Wilkins tentatively proposes a simple model for penalty determination

$$P = fC + (A - M)$$

where P is punishment, C is crime seriousness, and A and M assessments of aggravation and mitigation respectively. Against this can be placed the implicit model of Thomas, which is

$$P = fC - M$$

Looking at the list reproduced as Table 10, Wilkins remarks:

It is interesting to note the lack of balance between the categories, despite the fact that respondents were asked to add items they thought should be included. The lack of balance does not appear to be due to the nature of the categorisation chosen but to be a reflection of the population of ideas that were sampled by the questions.

What is the nature of the imbalance? It could be argued that few of the factors in mitigation concern the crime act and its immediate context (only two are clearly so related: offender's drinking at the time of the crime and the likelihood of provocation) whereas of the aggravating factors at least half are concerned with the immediate crime in context, arguably as many as three-quarters. The reader is invited to make his own decision after inspection of Table 10. On balance, then, there is some suggestion that aggravation tends to operate on the perception of the act and mitigation on the perception of the offender. This view may have enough merit to justify further research.

Wilkins went on to ask groups of people, for each reason of mitigation or aggravation, to rate the reason 'as a justified cause of reduction (increase in the case of aggravating factors) of penalty on the 1–8 scale'. The groups of people he used must set some sort of record for diversity, since it included Canadian judges, West Canadian students, Eastern US students, US police, participants in an international (United Nations) seminar in Tokyo, and research staff of a US national crime research organisation. He found high consensus (at the group level) between his groups on aggravating factors, and substantial, albeit much lower, consensus, in regard to mitigating factors. The most important aggravating factors tended to be those associated with the crime act itself. So in both the balance of items and the relative agreed importance in the degree of aggravation which aggravating factors represent, aggravation tends to be act- rather than actor-derived.

What factors are mitigating?

Thomas's (1979a) review of the decisions of the Court of Appeal yields a number of factors stated to be mitigating. These overlap substantially with the mitigating factors identified by Wilkins (see above) and those identified by Shapland (1981) as occurring frequently in speeches

Table 10 *Listing of aggravating and mitigating factors*

Aggravating factors	Mitigating factors
Offender continued criminal activity after arrest	Offender is younger than usual for this crime
Offender showed erratic/irrational behaviour in the offence	Offender offers restitution
Offender showed bizarre/depraved behaviour in the offence	Offender assisted law officers in solving other crimes
Police state arrest was difficult	Offender has exceptionally good employment record
Offender under influence of drugs at time	Offender had been drinking at time
Offender under influence of alcohol at time	Offender of low intelligence
Offender a person of high status in community	Offender's wife a serious problem/family difficulties
Offender a person of no fixed abode	Prior mental treatment
Instant offence repeats an earlier	Physical handicap of offender
Instant offence is of different type from earlier	No arrests or convictions
Military record shows proven military crime	No arrests or convictions except as juvenile
Offender does not express remorse – e.g. found guilty but	No previous crimes of same kind
pleaded not guilty	No previous crimes, but only arrests
Victim was particularly vulnerable	Provocation seems likely
Injury to victim was unusually extensive	Victim is/was friend of offender
Damage to property was unusually extensive	Victim asks for leniency
Multiple injuries to victim	Political motive for crime
Victim is/was friend	Others involved apparently leaders
Victim is relation	Property recovered by police
Victim presses for heavy penalty	Prison would cause exceptional hardship to offender's dependants
Evidence of planning of the crime	
Much similar crime in district lately	

Source: Wilkins, 1983.

in mitigation and with factors mentioned in social inquiry reports (Thorpe, 1978), although both the Shapland and Thorpe lists are, as might be expected, considerably more extensive, since factors which the Court of Appeal has explicitly sanctioned as mitigating are only a subset of those likely to incline a court towards a merciful disposition.

Youth is 'one of the most effective mitigating factors' according to Thomas, as is the slightness of the criminal record, a gap in the criminal record, the offence out of character with the criminal record and evidence of good character, this last to the point of the oft-quoted case of Keightley who was rewarded by sentence reduction for having previously saved the life of a drowning child. Provocation, domestic, financial or emotional difficulties may mitigate sentence. Drink has little or no independent status as a mitigating factor in the eyes of the Court of Appeal, although indirect hardships to the offender's family or the offender himself through loss of a career may mitigate sentence, as may the experience or anticipation of special hardships in prison. Remorse, assistance to the police and the payment of compensation complete the list, with the sinister exception of 'grievances arising in the course of the proceedings' in which, for instance, undue delay or 'departure from proper standards of judicial behaviour' may allow relief from the otherwise appropriate sentence.

Shapland's (1981) detailed study of mitigation involved, *inter alia*, the analysis of the content of mitigation speeches. Table 11 reproduces those items which occurred in more than 10 per cent of speeches, ordered from most to least frequent. Most of the factors are recognisably mitigating from Thomas's list. Those concerning the offence itself occurred disproportionately where there was a guilty plea and hence no earlier opportunity to review the defendant's perspective on events.

One might expect a preponderance of mitigating factors being mentioned in social inquiry reports, given the traditional role of the probation service in the courts and the inclinations of probation officers to assist, as well as advise and befriend, offenders. Tables 12 and 13 are taken from Thorpe (1978). Table 12 shows the judged importance of different types of information to be found in social inquiry reports. As will be seen, the importance, particularly as judged by magistrates, reveals those factors identified by Thomas and Shapland to be at the top of the list. Table 13 is of particular interest in the context of mitigation. It lists the frequency of mention of topics in social inquiry reports according to whether the topic was mentioned

Table 11 *Mitigating factors mentioned in more than 10 per cent of 126 speeches in mitigation ranked by decreasing frequency of mention*

1	Has job / good job / in work now.
2	Good work record.
3	Minor role/part played by defendant.
4	Sorry/apologises/contrite.
5	Co-operated with police / admitted offence.
6	Settled relationship with family / family responsibilities.
7	No previous convictions.
8	Minor offence of its type.
9	Kept out of trouble since last conviction some time ago.
10	Relatives present in court.
11	Drink / judgment marred by drink.
12	Accepts must be punished / go to prison.
	Offers compensation.
14	Defendant was in financial difficulties.
	Has pleaded guilty.
16	Unlikely to do it again (view of others).
	In custody now.

Source: Shapland, 1981.

Table 12 *The importance of information in social inquiry reports measured by the order and frequency of choice of magistrates and probation officers*

Order of choice	Probation officers (120)	Frequency of choice	Magistrates (65)	Frequency of choice
1	Offence	119	Offence	65
2	Family relationships	111	Previous convictions	63
3	Parents and/or partner	101	Attitude to present offence	57
4	Previous convictions	116	Family relationships	48
5	Employment	112	Employment	59
6	Childhood	82	Parents and/or partner	48
7	Personality	102	Personality	43
8	Accommodation	90	Response to previous sentences	48
9	Brothers and sisters	78	Friends	36
10	Education	86	Medical history	44
11	Attitude to present offence	105	Drink and drugs	41
12	Medical history	86	Education	35
13	Family criminality	81	Childhood	32
14	Response to previous sentences	88	Intelligence	33
15	Marital/sexual situation	82	Finance	33
16	Friends	89	Interests and activities	34
17	Drink and drugs	83	Family criminality	33
18	Intelligence	77	Brothers and sisters	30
19	Interests and activities	89	Accommodation	32
20	Finance	71	Marital/sexual situation	31
21	–	–	Probation officers' recommendation	38

Source: Thorpe, 1978.

Table 13 *The extent to which topics in social inquiry reports were presented in a positive or favourable light as against a negative or unfavourable light (N = 467)*

Topic	Context in which topic mentioned		
	Positive favourable good	Negative unfavourable bad	No mention
Employment prospects	179	205	83
Employment history	188	188	91
Attitude to offence	263	42	162
Past attitude to work	219	84	164
Present attitude to work	236	58	173
Parental family stability	155	138	174
Relationship with parents	132	113	222
Condition of home	181	53	233
Stability of marital/sexual situation	146	55	266
Delinquency of friends	78	94	295
Present attitude to supervision	120	44	303
Past attitude to school	85	61	321
Past attitude to supervision	81	58	328
Leisure	62	32	373
Influence of partner	74	15	378
Intelligence	29	56	271[a]
Past attitude to custody	42	27	398
Ability to form relationships	17	30	420
Sibling delinquency	23	21	423

Note

[a] Excludes 111 cases where intelligence was described as 'average'.

Source: Thorpe, 1978.

in a light favourable or unfavourable to the offender. Inspection of the table shows:

(1) That the extent to which topics are not mentioned is enormous. Clearly information is selected as relevant to the probation officer's purpose in a particular case from a much wider repertoire.

(2) When information is selected for inclusion in a social inquiry report, it is predominantly favourable to the defendant.

(3) Most topics whose mentions are predominantly favourable to the offender are recognisable as the factors in mitigation identified by Shapland (1981).

(4) Those topics whose mentions are predominantly unfavourable to the offender are in effect sad tales, e.g. a man with poor employment prospects, delinquent friends and an inability to form relationships.

The evidence reviewed inclines us to the view that aggravation operates primarily on the view of the offence and that mitigation operates primarily on the view of the offender, but this is more of a suspicion in a complex area than a belief, at least for the United Kingdom. The Wilkins data are not British, and only they present data about aggravation. Mitigation is more visible in legal process. We all have sad tales to tell, which do not require a lawyer's time and expertise to express. Perhaps mitigation is so often offender-based because it is the path of least effort towards sympathy. Perhaps it is because offence-based mitigations are so specific to the situation that they do not cross the frequency threshold necessary for their inclusion in Tables 11–13.

We must not conclude that the repertoire of mitigations is a common-sense set of excuses or justifications. Shapland (1981) shows that there is indeed overlap between conventional excuses and excuses offered in mitigation, but she also notes differences flowing from differences of formality of context, time lapse between event and excuse, preclusion of possible excuses used in making a defence, and so on. Her demonstration of how inept unrepresented defendants are in making speeches in mitigation is of great practical importance, as is her finding that barristers vary in the information they use to construct a plea in mitigation. But even if one accepts everything written in this chapter so far, although we now have some awareness of the vocabulary of mitigation, we do not understand how it is articulated into sentencing.

Where does mitigation start?

Thomas (1979a), as we have noted earlier, argues that the first two steps in calculating a tariff sentence involve defining a scale of sentences in relation to typical instances of an offence, and placing the facts of the case on that scale. These two steps precede sentence reduction by mitigation. One factor agreed by all to be relevant to the grant or withholding of mitigation is criminal history. The longer and more regular one's pattern of recorded offending, the less mitigation one can expect. This progressive loss of mitigation continues to the point at which there is no mitigation left to be lost.

Ashworth (1983), in a closely argued chapter whose title 'Punishing Persistence' points to the central difficulty we are to discuss, shows that there are views of sentencing which would yield sentencing practices which are largely indistinguishable from those which would result from the application of progressive loss of remission. For example the principle of cumulative sentencing would lead to more severe sentences for those with worse criminal records, as would progressive loss of mitigation. The difference between the two principles would show itself only when the lack of a ceiling in cumulative sentencing led to those with the very worst criminal records being sentenced more severely than those with only slightly better records. In the abstract, then, the two principles do have a crucial test of difference, that length of record beyond a particular level should be irrelevant under progressive loss of mitigation but not under cumulative sentencing. Philpotts and Lancucki (1979) have produced the most detailed evidence available on the relationship between sentence and previous convictions. Table 14, reproduced from their report, shows the relevant breakdown by sex of offender. It will be evident from this table that the proportion of the sample given custodial sentences

Table 14 *Persons convicted of standard list offences in January 1971, by sex, number of previous convictions and sentence*

Number of convictions prior to January 1971	Total number of persons	Sentence in January 1971 (% of total number of persons)					
		Discharge	Fine	Probation or supervision	Suspended sentence	Custodial sentence	Other sentence
Males							
0	2,060	16	65	8	3	3	4
1	784	7	52	13	10	12	6
2 to 4	1,054	6	41	11	12	26	4
5 or more	527	4	25	7	14	47	2
Total	4,425	11	52	9	8	16	4
Females							
0	433	24	58	13	2	1	2
1 or more	142	18	37	18	13	9	4
Total	575	23	53	14	5	3	2

Source: Philpotts and Lancucki, 1979.

increases as number of previous convictions increases. Males with no previous convictions are given active custody 3 per cent of the time, those with five or more previous convictions were given custodial sentences 47 per cent of the time. This pattern reproduces itself when offenders are divided according to age and by offence-type.

If progressive loss of mitigation works, it operates on either an absolute or a proportional basis. If absolute, every extra offence costs a constant amount of the available credit, up to the point at which no credit is left. On this view, the same amount of mitigation is lost by having n rather than n-1 convictions, so long as n does not exceed the number where credit has run out, whatever the value of n. A more plausible view is that progressive loss of mitigation works on proportions, so that a constant proportion of available credit is expended in every extra conviction. On such a view, the amount of mitigation lost by having three rather than two previous convictions is less than the amount lost by having one rather than no previous convictions. If progressive loss of mitigation does work in this way, it is in principle cumulative sentencing, but the sentencing differentials would become so slight with long criminal careers as to be imperceptible. Assuming progressive loss of mitigation on a proportional basis, we decided to apply a linear regression analysis to the Philpotts and Lancucki data. We recognise the spectacular crudity of this analysis with the data at hand, but we simply wish to illustrate how the issue of distinguishing between the alternatives could be addressed.

Looking at data elsewhere in the Philpotts and Lancucki report, it is evident that the actual average (median) number of convictions in the 2−4 previous conviction band is 3.43 and in the 5 + band 6.93. We thus calculated a regression equation for the first three pairs of data points (0,3; 1,12; 3.43,26) and asked what, on the basis of that equation, would be the predicted rate of custody use with 6.93 previous convictions. Clearly, if the data show proportional progressive loss of mitigation, the predicted use of custody should be well above the actual use of custody. If cumulative sentencing is occurring, the equation would (?) accurately predict custody use. In fact the custody use predicted by the equation is 49, remarkably close to the 47 per cent to be found in Philpotts and Lancucki's data.

To be at all persuasive, this analysis should be done on an offence-by-offence basis, which is not possible with the Philpotts and

Lancucki data, and with data on sentence length. Nevertheless this crude approach leaves open the real possibility that current sentence practice approximates more closely to cumulative sentencing practice than to progressive loss of mitigation. It should also be borne in mind that the proportion of serious instant offences provides a natural limit to custody use which, it may be hazarded, would push the analysis towards a pattern interpretable as progressive loss of mitigation, which still did not appear.

The only other mitigating variable on which research relevant to the incorporation of mitigation into sentencing generally comes from the investigation of guilty pleas. These are associated with a sentencing discount, in principle because they show remorse (Thomas, 1979a). Ashworth (1983) argues powerfully against this discount. Evidence which may be taken as supportive of Ashworth's position comes from Baldwin and McConville (1978). They studied cases in Birmingham Crown Court, being interested in comparisons between those who pleaded guilty consistently, those who changed their plea from not guilty to guilty, and those who consistently pleaded guilty. Baldwin and McConville matched their samples to control for those factors likely to affect markedly the severity of sentence imposed. The general view they have expressed in other publications is that late change of plea indicates completion of some kind of deal or understanding to exchange a guilty plea for a lenient sentence. Tables 15 and 16 are reproduced from the Baldwin and McConville (1978) paper. Both tables show that there is indeed a sentencing discount for a guilty plea.

Table 15 *Sentences imposed on defendants according to plea*

	Late plea-changers (n = 150)		Guilty pleas (n = 150)		Convicted after not guilty plea (n = 150)	
	%		%		%	
Absolute or conditional discharge	10.0		5.3		4.0	
Fine	10.7	57.4	9.3	50.0	6.7	30.7
Probation	12.0		11.4		2.7	
Suspended sentence	24.7		24.0		17.3	
Prison sentence	35.9	42.6	44.7	50.0	57.3	69.3
Other custodial sentence (e.g. Borstal)	6.7		5.3		12.0	
	100.0		100.0		100.0	

Source: Baldwin and McConville, 1978.

Table 16 *Length of custodial sentences according to plea*

	Late plea-changers	Guilty pleas	Convicted after not-guilty plea
	%	%	%
Not relevant – defendant given a non-custodial sentence	57.4	50.0	30.7
Custodial sentence:			
less than 12 months	12.0	10.0	24.7
1 year to less than 3 years	25.3	22.7	26.6
3 years or more	5.3	17.3	18.0
	100.0	100.0	100.0

Source: Baldwin and McConville, 1978.

They also show that there is an even greater discount for late change of plea. This is true both for the imposition of a custodial rather than a non-custodial sentence and for the length of the sentence once imposed. Can it be that people who change their plea show even greater remorse than people who consistently plead guilty? This is scarcely credible. It seems more likely that the Baldwin and McConville study shows at least one hidden mitigating factor, the willingness to save court time.

A footnote on mitigation thinking

In the latter half of this chapter we have been concerned to keep the discussion closer to court practice than is the case elsewhere in the book. However, we will not neglect completely the discussion of one strand of thinking in cognitive psychology which is relevant to mitigation, and particularly relevant to 'sad tale' mitigation. Mitigation requires causal thinking. For example, one mitigating factor (in Wilkins' list) is 'Offender's wife a serious problem / family difficulties'. Such a piece of information is only mitigating in effect if it caused the person's greater vulnerability to temptation to commit an offence. Consider the following problem, taken from Tversky and Kahneman (1982):

Which of the following events is more probable?
(a) that a girl has blue eyes if her mother has blue eyes
(b) that the mother has blue eyes if her daughter has blue eyes
(c) that the two events are equally probable.

Despite the availability of the (correct) alternative (c) three times as many people were prepared to agree with alternative (a) as with alternative (b). They were also more confident in predictions of weight from height than height from weight, and saw North Korea as more similar to China than China was similar to North Korea! In short there is 'inferential asymmetry' such that the more focal an event is, the greater relationship other events are seen as having to it. In mitigation, crime is the focal event, and therefore the prior event is seen as causal of the crime more than the crime is seen as diagnostic of the prior event. To expand our example, the offender robbed a shopkeeper because he had trouble with his wife, rather than the kind of person who robs a bank is also likely to have had trouble with his wife. The general view is that the relationship between drug use and crime is one in which crime is committed to feed a drug habit. Yet as Wardlaw (1978) points out: 'A substantial proportion of drug users commit criminal offences prior to addiction or heavy drug use, a finding that casts serious doubt on the widely held belief that drug use is a major cause of crime.' This may be illustrated by reference to another of Tversky and Kahneman's problems:

Which of the two probabilities is higher? The probability that there will be rationing of fuel for individual consumers in the US during the 1990s, if you assume that a marked increase in the use of solar energy for home heating will occur during the 1980s. OR the probability that there will be rationing of fuel for individual consumers in the US during the 1990s, if you assume that no marked increase in the use of solar energy for home heating will occur during the 1980s.

Most people argue that the first alternative is more probable. This is because they take rationing as the focal event and give the increase in use of solar energy as causal. As Tversky and Kahneman argue:

The event that there will be a marked increase in the use of solar energy for home heating during the 1980s has both causal and diagnostic significance ... Other things being equal, a marked increase in the use of solar energy can only alleviate a fuel crisis in later years. However a marked increase in the use of solar energy during the 80s also provides a strong indication of an impending energy crisis. In particular, it suggests that fuel prices in the 80s are sufficiently high to make the investment in solar energy for home heating economical for a large number of consumers.

Similarly, marriage problems may as readily be seen as the result of being an intolerable person as the cause of a subsequent offence. Yet implied causal links are used in *mitigation*. In short, it may be that an understanding of inferential asymmetry may quite undermine many of the assumptions underlying conventional thinking on mitigation.

CHAPTER 9

The arithmetic of imprisonment and the psychology of imprisoning

The next two chapters of the book change the focus of concern. To this point, the emphasis has been on the enunciation of principles derived from the work of psychologists and speculation on the implications of those for sentencing theory and practice. In the next two chapters, the starting-point will be problems recognised by practitioners of criminal justice, and attempts will be made to cite psychological and other social science research relevant to these problems. Because it is important for psychologists not to be constrained within an area defined by criminal justice personnel, the emphasis to this point is not regretted. However it seems important to address issues of sentence from at least some of the perspectives current in criminal justice. Even these perspectives will be more familiar in the corridors of the Home Office than of the Old Bailey, if for no other reason than that the present pattern of sentencing is seen to be more problematic by those in the Home Office.

The two topics to be dealt with are, first, the sentence of imprisonment, and second, the issue of disparity.

The use of imprisonment

The Home Office *Review of Criminal Justice Policy*, published in 1977, stated that the reduction of the prison population was a 'particular preoccupation' of the Home Office. In the same year, a Conservative Party Study Report agreed that 'there is an urgent need now to reduce the prison population where this can be done without putting at risk the safety of the general public'. Baldock (1980) asserted, 'It is almost universally agreed that the prison population in this country has grown too large, continues to grow and ought to be reduced.' It is clear from the pronouncements of politicians since that time that they at least were accurately represented by Baldock.

The Parliamentary All-Party Penal Affairs Group's 1980 report makes this most explicit, together with the views of the House of Commons Expenditure Committee dealing with prisons, also published in 1980. It would be tedious to rehearse the long list of expressions of opinion in recent years that the prison population is too large. At the time of writing, we await a decision on proposals for the introduction of intermittent custody, yet another attempt to divert from imprisonment which bespeaks the continuing concern of government to reduce the size of the prison population.

How to reduce the prison population

If one wishes to reduce the prison population there are two, and only two, ways of doing it. You either imprison fewer people, or you imprison the same number of people for a shorter time (or you can do both). Of course these approaches are likely to be interdependent. For example, if one were to reduce sentence lengths generally, it seems plausible that the shortest-sentence prisoners would drop into non-custodial categories, and if one succeeded in removing all prisoners from short periods of custody (say 0–3 months) into non-custodial sentences, it seems unlikely that the prison sentence band 0–3 months would remain empty, and probable that people would drop from the longer-sentence bands into the 0–3 months band. Nonetheless, the two strategies, of shortening sentences on the one hand and diverting from custody on the other, can be regarded as independent, and treated in turn. This is because the consequences of the strategies (in any realistically envisagable form) for the size of the prison population are so different.

Reducing the prison population by the increased use of non-custodial sentences

With the important exception of the introduction of parole and its subsequent expansion, the major thrust has been to replace the use of custodial by non-custodial sentences. The introduction since 1967 of suspended sentences, partly suspended sentences, supervised suspended sentences, community service orders, deferred sentences, probation orders with condition of attendance at a day training centre, and restrictions on the imposition of a first prison sentence are all directed at reducing the use of imprisonment.

A strategy for reducing the prison population must take four factors into account:

(1) The number of different decisions (i.e. non-custodial) which would have to be made to have a non-trivial impact on the size of the prison population would be enormous. Table 17 illustrates this.

Table 17 *Receptions under sentence, 1980[a] (adult males without the option of fine payment)*

Sentence bands in months[b]	Receptions	Average effective sentence length in years	Implied population
$x \leq 3$	7,112	0·16	114
$3 < x \leq 6$	7,141	0·25	1,786
$6 < x > 18$	8,749	0·54	4,724
18	2,296	1·00	2,296
$18 < x \leq 48$	5,633	1·49	8,393
$48 < x \leq 120$	982	3·21	3,152
$x > 120$	54	8·00	432
Life	162	10·00	1,620
Total	32,130		22,517

Note

(a) The year is chosen as typical.

(b) For example the band $3 < x \leq 6$ refers to sentences of above 3 months but less than or equal to six months.

The left-hand column represents sentence-length bands illustrated in prison statistics. The third column illustrates the average effective length of these sentences, in years, making estimates of remission and parole use based on information in prison statistics, and assuming all sentences to lie at the midpoint of the band in the left-hand column. The approximations tend not seriously to distort the picture (see Pease, 1980). The second column shows the annual number of receptions in the relevant sentence band, and the right-hand column the approximate number of people serving sentences within that band who are in prison at any one time. Thus it can be seen that to reduce the prison population by a modest 114 one would have to avoid, by means of a different sentencing decision, 7, space 112 receptions. Sentencing all 14,254 adult males who currently get sentences of six months or less to non-custodial measures instead would reduce the prison population by less than 2,000 — and this is an overestimate, because of the next issue to be dealt with.

(2) Short-sentence prisoners are reconvicted more quickly and in a greater proportion of cases than are longer-sentence prisoners. Thus one-quarter of those discharged from prison sentences of between three and six months are re-imprisoned within two years of release, compared with around 15 per cent of those discharged from sentences of all lengths. This, of course, means that the actual reduction in prison population would be even less than the modest saving described earlier, and would be attended by a substantial increase in police and court business.

(3) Sentencers' enthusiasm to replace custodial by non-custodial measures cannot be taken for granted. To quote Su Fairhead (1981), writing about persistent petty offenders:

On the one hand the results suggested that magistrates were in general satisfied with their sentencing decisions, even when awarding imprisonment. They were least likely to be satisfied when the offender was homeless but their dissatis-faction was more likely to stem from being unable to impose heavier penalties than from having limited options for non-custodial alternatives.

(4) Finally, and perhaps most importantly, recent experience suggests that, to put it at its lowest, not all cases attracting sentences intended as alternatives to active custody would otherwise have been given active custodial sentences (and, in the case of suspended sentences, active custodial sentences of the same length). To summarise the experience of diversion from custody, such diversion as has been achieved has taken place at the cost of confusion and attendant injustice. Because of its importance in understanding the psychology of judicial sentencing as it relates to imprisonment, the fate of 'alternatives to imprisonment' will be considered at some length.

The non-custodial alternative to imprisonment

Suspended sentences of imprisonment were enacted in 1967. These were in law sentences of imprisonment to be imposed only where sentences of imprisonment were appropriate. In the definitive *O'Keefe* judgment ([1969] 2 QB 29) judges were directed that in each case they must decide first that a sentence of imprisonment is required, and subsequently whether it could be suspended. That is to say, a suspended sentence should only be imposed when, having eliminated all other alternatives, the court decides that the case is one for imprisonment, the final question being, given that imprisonment is unavoidable, can it be avoided by suspension! The sense is clear, although the psychology which it implies is tortured. Sparks (1971) estimated from distributions of sentences passed that 40−55 per cent of those given suspended sentences in 1968−9 had escaped custody. Oatham and Simon (1972) showed that 'courts have used the suspended sentence both to replace immediate imprisonment and as a sentence in its own right ... It has been estimated that of all persons awarded a suspended sentence, only somewhere between 40 per cent and 50 per cent would, but for the new provision, have been sentenced to imprisonment.' Sebba (1969) found in Israeli district courts that suspended sentences were used in place of fines in half of the cases in which they were used. Bottoms (1981) reviews the 'malfunction' of suspended sentence use. Shapland (1981) in her study of mitigation happens to reproduce a transcript of a case which perfectly illustrates the point. At an early point in the transcript the sentencer informs defence counsel, 'If it will assist you in any way, I don't contemplate custody; I don't have it in mind to send them to prison.' Later, the sentencer imposes a three-month suspended sentence of imprisonment.

The same malfunction evident in the wholly suspended sentence is now becoming evident for the partly suspended sentence. An assessment of its use published in Criminal Statistics (England and Wales) 1982 suggests that the partly suspended sentence is being used about half the time as an alternative to a wholly non-custodial sentence (including the fully suspended sentence) and half the time as an alternative to a wholly custodial sentence. This means that the attempt to divert people from custody has at least in this case diverted people directly into custody.

The community service order was, together with the suspended sentence, perhaps the most important attempt to divert from custody attempted in England and Wales during the last twenty years. Politicians in the debates leading to the passing of the 1972 Criminal Justice Act made pronouncements like, 'I was attracted from the start by the idea that people who had committed a minor offence would be better occupied doing a service to their fellow citizens than sitting alongside others in a crowded gaol', and 'The alternative would be to go to gaol.' The 1974 Home Office Circular giving guidance to the courts about the use of community service orders suggested that the use of the order instead of another non-custodial sentence would be 'occasional'. Yet various commentators have estimated that the use of community service orders to replace other non-custodial sentences in England and Wales has been substantial (Young, 1979; Willis, 1977), being estimated at around 50 per cent in England and Wales (Pease *et al.*, 1977) and slightly less in Scotland (Duguid, 1982).

Estimates of use of community service orders ('work orders') in some Australian states are very similar to the British ones. In Tasmania, the Probation of Offenders Act 1971 made clear the intended substitution of work orders for imprisonment. 'Instead of sentencing a person to undergo a term of imprisonment, the Supreme Court and courts of summary jurisdiction may, with the person's consent, adjudge that he for his offence attend at such places and times as shall be notified to him in writing by a probation officer or a supervisor on so many Saturdays, not exceeding 25, as the court may order.' Despite the clarity of this intention, it is clear (Mackay and Rook, 1976; Rook, 1978a, b) that around half of those given orders would otherwise have been given other non-custodial sentences. Educated guesses about similar proportions come from other Australian states, Victoria and New South Wales. A guess from the Canadian province of Ontario is vague but compatible:

Initially, community service orders were intended to provide an alternative sentence to the incarceration of offenders. Because of the low-risk nature of this CSO client population, however, it is unlikely that the CSO option is constituting an alternative to incarceration too extensively. These probationers probably would not have otherwise been sentenced to a term of incarceration. (Polonoski, 1981)

A similarly well-informed view is expressed about community service orders in the United States (Harland, 1981).

Apart from the case of the partly suspended sentence, however, the sentences discussed have diverted some people *from* custody. Given the brevity of the prison sentences which those really diverted would have received, the effective reduction in the size of the prison population is certain to be slight.

There is scope for confusion between participants in the court process about the place of an 'alternative to custody' within the range of alternative sentences. For example, a court revoking an alternative to custody may substitute a prison sentence even when it was not intended by the court originally imposing the alternative. A significant 1977 decision of the Appeal Court (3442/C/77) held that:

when a community service order is made, it saves the person in respect of whom it was made from an immediate custodial sentence. It is to that extent an indulgence to him ... if the order is not complied with, those who break the terms of the order cannot complain if a custodial sentence is imposed, when they have thrown away the advantage which was offered to them.

But what if the order were one of the half of orders not made as an alternative to custody? The Appeal Court decision increases the possibility of prison being endured for an offence not originally thought to merit it. Further, it is not without significance that whenever offenders on community service have been asked what sentence they would have received if community service orders had been unavailable, they always estimate custody in a higher proportion of cases than is realistic (Flegg *et al.*, 1976; Whittington, 1977; Parker, 1980; Polonoski, 1980). It is thus certain that they consent to orders on an unrealistic view of what would otherwise be imposed.

Vass (1984) provides much evidence that the position of community service as, in principle, an alternative to custody, is used by magistrates and others to enforce co-operation. He quotes a magistrate: '[The offender] does not know our intentions. This is part of the game ... He may not like [community service] but he accepts because of fear of the alternative which he associates with imprisonment'; and a probation officer: 'I do not consider community service as an alternative [to prison] ... At interviews we always tell community service workers that the order is an alternative .. We have to ... Vetting and consent could prove disastrous if fear of imprisonment was not present.'

The Lord Chief Justice, Lord Lane, has produced guidelines for the maze of sentences around the threshold of custody (*R.* v. *Clarke*, [1982] Crim. L.R. 464) which merit discussion.

Before imposing a partly suspended sentence the court should ask itself the following question: first of all, is this a case where a custodial sentence is really necessary? If it is not, it should pass a non-custodial sentence. But if it is necessary, then the court should ask itself secondly this: can we make a community service order as an equivalent to imprisonment, or can we suspend the whole sentence? If not, then the point arises: what is the shortest sentence the court can properly impose? In many cases, of which an obvious example is the case of the first offender for whom a short term of imprisonment is a sufficient shock, without any suspension, that would be enough. If imprisonment is necessary, and if a very short sentence is not enough, and if it is not appropriate to suspend the sentence altogether, then partial suspension should be considered ... In general the type of case that we have in mind is where the gravity of the offence is such that at least six months' imprisonment is merited, but where there are mitigating circumstances which point towards a measure of leniency not sufficient to warrant total suspension.

The niceties of judgment and leaps of imagination which such a prescription requires are unlikely to be found even in so august a group as judges.

Expressed as a flow chart (see Figure 6), certain features of Lord Lane's advice become clear.

(1) Community service and the suspended sentence must be considered only after a custodial sentence has been judged necessary.
(2) Community service (involving up to 240 hours' work) is implicitly down-tariff of the suspended sentence (which involves only a threat).
(3) Mitigation is first mentioned in relation to partly suspended sentences. It is not mentioned in relation to whether a custodial sentence is necessary in the first place nor in any of the decisions preceding the decision on part-suspension.

One gets a sense of unreality from Lord Lane's commendable attempt to plot a path through a sentencing minefield. Let us take the notion, for example, that the decision that imprisonment is necessary must anticipate the decision to allow the offender to escape imprisonment by one means or another. This implies a scale of equivalences inconsistent with almost anyone's views of such a scale. The notion that mitigation first presents itself so late in the day conflicts with general views of mitigation. If it is intended that mitigation should be used earlier (and it is probable that Lord Lane intended this but was concentrating on part-suspension in his guidance) one must ask what subset of mitigation becomes relevant which has not been fully taken into account earlier in the process.

For a different view of the partly suspended sentence, there are the thoughts of its original advocate in Parliament, Mr Patrick Mayhew, who during the debates leading up to the 1977 Act said of the partly suspended sentence, 'It is important that it should be seen not as providing a soft option but as providing an option that will enable the courts to deal more severely than they often feel able to now with people who need to have the deterrence of a taste of prison.' That cannot mean anything other than the imposition of longer sentences when part is suspended than when it is not.

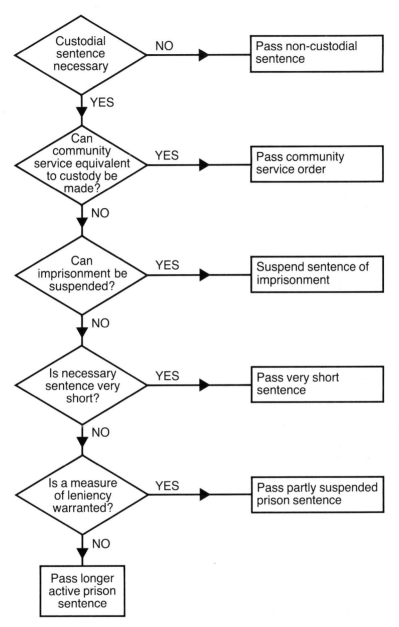

Figure 6 Flow chart representing Lord Lane's advice on part-suspension of prison sentences

In short, we feel justified in our earlier conclusion about attempts to reduce the prison population by the introduction of alternatives to custody, namely that such slight diversion as has been achieved has been achieved at the cost of confusion and attendant injustice.

Reducing the prison population by reducing sentence lengths

Reducing sentence lengths has an almost directly proportional effect in reducing the prison population. A 10 per cent reduction in sentence length would effect approximately a 9.5 per cent reduction in the sentenced population, taking into account swifter reconviction and re-imprisonment. Looking again at the group identified in Table 17, adult male prisoners sentenced without the option of fine, that would represent a greater reduction than diverting all those sentenced to six months or less, all 14,254 of them.

The crucial question is, of course, how to achieve such a reduction in average sentence length. The Parliamentary All-Party Penal Affairs Group, in its 1981 document *Still Too Many Prisoners*, argues that attempts to persuade the courts to pass shorter sentences have not been successful. In the whole post-war period this may be unfair, but the tenour of the debate in recent years certainly suggests that the scope for successful voluntary reduction of sentence lengths by courts is slight or non-existent. Even the widely known *Upton* and *Bibi* judgments (see Ashworth, 1983) of the Appeal Court, whose incorporation into sentencing practice would yield a reduction of sentence length, appear to have been without perceptible effect (see Prison Statistics 1982, England and Wales). Reduction of sentence length must come, it seems, through executive action, it if is come from anywhere.

The difficulty is that any conventional initiative of this kind can be rendered ineffective by courts simply increasing the length of the sentences they impose. There is no clear evidence that the courts have done this in either of the two relevant initiatives of the last twenty years, conditional release in Northern Ireland and parole in England and Wales. However, lengthening of sentences in Northern Ireland after conditional release cannot be entirely explained by change in patterns of offending (see Northern Ireland Office, 1984), and in England and Wales the average number of determinate sentences of ten years or more in the period 1964–8 was fifty-eight, compared with eighty in the years 1969–72. This is at least consistent with the view that judges were determined to ensure a long prison stay for those whom they regarded as particularly serious offenders, and extended sentence length accordingly. However, as is clear from Walker (1981) there was no overall increase in sentence length consequent upon the introduction of parole in England and Wales.

Whatever one's conclusions about judicial lengthening of sentences accompanying executive shortening of sentences, the fact remains that judges could choose to subvert executive purpose in this way. We concluded above that executive reduction of average sentence length is much the best hope for worthwhile reduction in the prison population. So is there a way to do this which is not susceptible to sabotage by judges? There is a way, but one which requires a fundamentally different way of thinking about the relationship between sentencing and prison population. The basic idea involves using system capacity as a determinant of how long people stay in prison. We are accustomed to think of the prison population as determined by the behaviour of judges with the rest of us as helpless bystanders. But it need not be so. Justice inheres in proportionality between culpability and sentence severity, but it does not imply a constant level of punishment across time (otherwise we would still be transporting people, if we could find anywhere to take them). If a sentence could leave that proportionality untouched, but reduce sentence lengths across the board, that would satisfy our concerns, both for justice and for a smaller prison population.

Such a scheme could take the form of a sliding scale of remission. The process would be one in which Parliament decides the size of prison population the country could afford, and the rate of remission is continually adjusted so that that population is never exceeded. So if, for example, the sentencing practice of the courts would yield a prison population which is, say, 2,000 above the target population, the proportion of the sentence remitted for good behaviour is increased by the amount necessary, say 5 per cent, to yield the target population. Parliament simply specifies the target population, and the process after that is automatic. That would mean that however much judges increased the lengths of their sentences, the target prison population would never be exceeded. Clearly there would have to be refinements of the scheme in the interests of justice. For example, if sentences became more lenient after a prisoner was sentenced, it is unreasonable for his expected date of release to move further away into the future, so a ratchet principle should operate, whereby changes in sentencing practice during a prisoner's sentence could advance his release data but not retard it.

The sliding scale of remission may not quite yet be practical politics (although the reduction of the effective length of Borstal training as number of receptions increased is a *de facto* sliding scale of remission), but it is not pure expediency. It has the advantage that it could be guaranteed to reduce the prison population by any desired amount without seriously violating proportionality between crime and punishment. Aside from that, it would focus attention on the options we forgo by spending a fortune on maintaining a high prison population. There is now no occasion on which the options can be connected as options. The annual rebate in Parliament on setting the target population would afford just such an opportunity, as the Budget debate allows discussion of fiscal policy alternatives.

Legislation for motivation

Wherein lies the wisdom of Solomon? Surely it lies in where he directed his attention. In deciding a custody case, he made appeal not to the facts of the case but to the motives which underlay them. River pollution by industry could be reduced by requiring factories to take in water for processes downstream from the factory's outflow. Be they ever so public-spirited, judges too can have their behaviour modified by providing incentives to behave differently. When a Home Secretary tells the Commons (H.C. Deb., 20, 22), 'We are determined to ensure that there will be room in the prison system for every person whom the judges and magistrates decide should go there, and we will continue to do whatever is necessary for that purpose', this does not provide a powerful incentive for courts to restrict their use of imprisonment. Two imaginative schemes have attempted to provide a financial incentive to sentencers to decrease their use of custody.

The first was the California Probation Subsidy. The California State Board of Corrections concluded in 1964 that the level of non-custodial treatment of offenders was too low, which they attributed to the low level of probation provision (California Youth Authority, 1975, 1977). However, the Board reasoned that the state legislature might be persuaded to allocate money if there were a built-in method of ensuring that fewer people were sent to prison so that extra probation expenditure would be matched by savings in the custodial budget. Counties in California opted into the programme, and each county's earnings were calculated in proportion to the amount by which its commitments to prison declined. The Probation Subsidy programme used a statutory formula to determine a participating county's 'earnings'. Participation by the counties was entirely voluntary. Earnings were based on a county's reduction of adult and juvenile commitments to the State Department of Corrections and the Department of the Youth Authority.

The benchmark from which a county's 'earnings' were computed was its own past commitment performance over a five-year period beginning in 1959 and continuing through 1963, or the two years 1962–3, whichever was higher. This five-year or two-year average commitment rate yielded a constant 'base commitment rate' for the county. Annually, this rate was applied against the county's population to determine its 'expected number of commitments'. A county was entitled to subvention if its total commitments for any given year were less than its expected number of commitments. The amount of subvention was dependent upon a formula that provided varied amounts from $2,080 to $4,000 per case, with the larger amounts taking effect as counties reduce more. In general, counties with a relatively low base commitment rate needed only to reduce commitments by 5 per cent to reach the $4,000 figure, while counties with high base commitment rates needed to reduce by as much as 25 per cent to achieve the same figure.

From the introduction of the scheme in 1966 to 1971 it was estimated that the scheme had saved California $126,000,000. By 1973 the number of commitments to state institutions by participating counties had been halved. The development of probation subsidy in California was stopped by the enactment of determinate sentencing policy. Its manner of operation has been criticised, and received criminological wisdom tends to suggest that the scheme failed (Lerman, 1975). However, the criticisms are contradictory (the police complaining about the reduction of custody which some academics deny was occurring). Certainly there were features of the scheme in operation which were not conducive to success. For example, if subsidy is based on commitments to custody, taking no account of length of time served, it is all too possible for there to be no net decrease in the use of custody. Further, the possibility of combining probation with custody in local jails for periods of up to one year, possibly as an alternative to a period of just over a year in state institutions, causes problems. Incarceration in local jails does not count as incarceration for subsidy purposes, since there is no charge on the state. To a certain extent, therefore, the subsidy simply shifts the carceral population into local jails from state prisons. However, there is nothing in the criticisms of the California subsidy scheme which is of such importance as to make it unworthy of further consideration. It was the first, ingenious attempt to exploit a motive in the penal sphere. Any future scheme along the same lines must incorporate sentence length as well as the initial decision to incarcerate, given the earlier observation about the crucial importance of sentence length as a determinant of the size of the prison population.

A second scheme of the same general type was enacted in Minnesota in 1973 as the Community Corrections Act (Minnesota Department of Corrections, 1979, 1980). Instead of rewarding the decreasing use of state custody, a direct subsidy is paid to participating counties. The catch is that participating counties are then charged for the use of state institutions for all adult offenders whose commitment offence carries a statutory maximum sentence of five yers or less, and are charged on a *per diem* basis for all commitments of juveniles to state facilities. Like the California subsidy scheme, the purpose of the Minnesota Community Corrections Act is the provision of incentives to sentencers to use less custody. Early signs are encouraging, but it may yet be that even the Minnesota formula may be wrong. However, as in the California scheme, a percentage of the subsidy must be used for the scheme's evaluation and when the evaluation research flows, it will not be lacking in interest. Any British scheme modelled on California or Minnesota will have to undergo a sea-change in order to stand any chance of success; a direct translation would presumably involve an increase in the rate support grant to participating areas, whose ratepayers then pay for prison space occupied by people from their area. This would not be seen as a direct motive to sentencers to change their behaviour, and would be a particularly heavy burden on ratepayers in inner-city areas. A variation could make use of a trade-off between police provision and prison provision, so that for every pound saved by an area through decreased use of custody, 50p be made available for extra policing. Clearly, policing could never be allowed to fall below a level thought to be adequate, but it could vary above that level, and this may serve as an incentive to courts.

Some readers may see both the American schemes described as invidious. Why not just bribe judges to let people off? Certainly one has to take the view initially that low levels of custodial sentencing are a good thing. British governments since 1960 have taken that view. Review of the criminological research which makes such a position reasonable is beyond the scope of this paper. Justice requires proportionality between culpability and sentence severity. That says nothing about the average level of sentences. Judges passing sentence are under pressure. Their sentencing practice responds to that pressure. It is no more immoral to change the general balance of pressures in the defendant's favour by financial means than to do so by providing him with legal representation. The general level of sentencing must surely be responsive to public policy. This is indeed the central theme of Ashworth (1983). It is incorporated into our penal system by the devices of remission and parole. It would be wrong to alter the balance for individual cases, but that was not what happened in either the California or the Minnesota schemes. The trick of motivating sentencers to avoid imprisonment has now been demonstrated, and there is no reason in principle why it should not be applied here.

Why has diversion by alternative sentences been tried so much?

One may reasonably ask oneself why the policy attempts to reduce the prison population have been so heavily directed towards generating new sentences as 'alternatives' to custody, given the demonstrable shortcomings of that approach. What is the aspect of political or judicial psychology which makes this sort of activity so apparently attractive? One possible reason is that the reduction of sentence length creates political problems attendant upon decisions to shorten the sentences of those who have committed serious crimes and been locked up for a long time. Another explanation employs the availability heuristic. Many Members of Parliament are lawyers by training. Only one, to our knowledge, has been a prison governor or prison officer. If one stands in court, one can see that most of those imprisoned are imprisoned for short periods. It would thus be understandable for those in court to conclude that (on the basis of the highly available image of their court experience) significant inroads into the prison population could be made by diverting short-term prisoners from custody. If MPs had been prison governors, with the image of the prison more available to them, it would be clear to them that the reduction of sentence length was the way to reduce the prison population, and there would be a different balance of attempts to reduce the population in favour of their more realistic view.

CHAPTER 10

A tide in the affairs of judges

At a recent international conference on psychology and law, a major address, delivered to a large and packed lecture theatre, was given, after a fulsome introduction, by Judge Christopher Oddie. In our few meetings with him, Judge Oddie impresses as an open-minded and shrewd observer of the judicial scene. We hope that he will forgive us for expressing the view that the ovation he received was only partly for the excellence of his address. It was as much for the fact that he was there at all, one of a small band of judges (which also includes Judges Clapham, Monier-Williams and Stockdale) responsive to the possible contributions of social science in general and psychology in particular to their work. Indifference or hostility to research is probably the more usual recent judicial response. The fate of the projected Oxford research has already been described. What has not been described in the Lord Chief Justice's reasons for refusal, from the standpoint of those refused:

> The Lord Chief Justice, Lord Lane, informed us that the research would not be allowed to go ahead. In his view it would not be worth the expenditure of judicial time and public money. He stated that many of the points we raised were well known among judges, and that further research on these issues would therefore be of no assistance to the judiciary. He denied that some of the more controversial practices which we reported, such as the listing policies in certain courts, were occurring, although he did go on to declare that if these practices were in fact taking place there they should not ... In his view the available textbooks give a fairly clear account of the factors which judges take into account in sentencing, and he could not think of any aspects of judicial sentencing upon which research might prove helpful. (Ashworth *et al.*, 1984)

Others are less sanguine about the state of sentencing (much of what has been written illustrates this). Ashworth (1983) proposes major reforms; Thomas (1983), writing of the Court of Appeal, bemoans the difficulty 'that the general body of the Court's decisions have become more erratic, more unpredictable and more inconsistent than they were throughout the 1960s and up to the mid to late 1970s, so that decisions which are carefully thought out in terms of principle are likely to be swamped by other decisions in which no principle is apparent, or a contradictory principle is adopted.' He continues, 'What is needed is the recognition that effective policy cannot be developed without adequate and accurate information, and that the view from the bench is not necessarily sufficiently comprehensive for this purpose.' Even the well-disposed Judge Oddie does not identify sentencing as one of the areas in which psychology has informed his practice (Oddie, 1984). The crucial sentence read: 'Psychological analysis of decision-making has long been a part of graduate business studies, and there can be few lawyers who would not enhance their knowledge of what actually happens in court by an acquaintance with some of the published research on legal decisions. *Jury* studies are of particular relevance to my own work in the Crown Court' (emphasis added).

In short, even if an application of psychological principles to sentencing is thought to be desirable, it does not seem timely to advocate it. Yet in Chapter 1 we argued that it was desirable, and here we will argue that, paradoxically, it is timely. Pressure towards change is evident in the dissatisfaction of responsible and eminent commentators like Thomas and Ashworth. Information about how victims want 'their' criminals punished is becoming available through the 1984 British Crime Survey (at the time of writing yet to be published). This must serve to point up discrepancies in reasoning or principles between victims and judges which judges may eventually feel obliged to address. Generally and imperceptibly, the moral focus of criminal justice is moving from the judge to the victim. Finally, and not least in importance, the organisation of psychologists into groups like the British Psychological Society's Division of Criminological and Legal Psychology serves to put before the legal profession accounts and examples of usable psychological research with which they may be more prepared than hitherto to engage.

Our book is a modest attempt to advance the process we have described above. In it we have argued that judges merit attention from psychologists. This is because of the importance of the judicial task, and to redress the imbalance of investigation which has emphasised the psychology of the powerless at the expense of the psychology of the powerful. It was argued that principles of sentencing are, by and large, not recognisable in sentencing practice, and that verbal statements of reasoning by judges is, although no doubt honest, likely to be unreliable. Many errors of reasoning are distinguished which are of relevance to the sentencing task, and their possible implications described. The literature on judgments of offence seriousness was reviewed and the concept found to be usable as a basis for retributive sentencing, on the grounds of broad social consensus as to seriousness. We have applied the elementary concepts of psychophysical scaling to judicial practice, and have speculated on psychological aspects of what are seen as major issues in sentencing practice, namely the use of imprisonment and disparities in sentencing.

In Chapter 1 we distinguished what we took to be two central issues which shaped our endeavours. These were the identification of general errors of reasoning and unwarranted sentence variation. We took the view that the identification of general reasoning principles was the more fundamental research task. To which of the many possibilities for development should priority now be given? We would particularly hope and argue for a dialogue between judges and psychologists to discuss the monitoring of judicial performance along the lines suggested in Chapter 6, and a study of the effects set out in Chapter 2, using judges as subjects. We found, in seeking to scale mitigation effects, two quite different ways of thinking about the principle of progressive loss of mitigation, with different practical significance (see Chapter 8). It may be that work of this kind could be carried out under the auspices of a Sentencing Council such as is advocated by Ashworth (1983). The improvement of understanding of judicial practice which this might, with good data, represent, is worth having.

Bibliography

Advisory Council on the Penal System (1977) *The Length of Prison Sentences.* London, HMSO.

Advisory Council on the Penal System (1978) *Sentences of Imprisonment: A Review of Maximum Penalties.* London, HMSO.

Ainsworth, P.B. and Pease K. (1981) Incapacitation Revisited. *Howard Journal*, 20, 160–9.

Akman D.D., Figlio R. and Normandeau A. (1967) Concerning the Measurement of Delinquency – A Rejoinder and Beyond. *British Journal of Criminology*, 7, 442–9.

Allen F. (1959) Criminal Justice, Legal Values and the Rehabilitative Ideal. *Journal of Criminal Law, Criminology and Police Science*, 50, 226–32.

Allen F. (1964) *The Borderland of Criminal Justice: Essays in Law and Criminology.* Chicago, University of Chicago Press.

Alpert W. and Raiffa H. (1982) A Progress Report on the Training of Probability Assessors. In Kahneman D., Slovic P. and Tversky A. (eds), *Judgment under Uncertainty: Heuristics and Biases.* Cambridge, Cambridge University Press.

Ashworth A. (1975) Sentencing: The Unintended Result. *Justice of the Peace*, 23 August, 480–1.

Ashworth A. (1977) Justifying the First Prison Sentence. *Criminal Law Review*, 661–73.

Ashworth A. (1983) *Sentencing and Penal Policy.* London, Weidenfeld & Nicolson.

Ashworth A. (1984) Techniques of Guidance on Sentencing. *Criminal Law Review*, September, 519–30.

Ashworth A., Genders E., Mansfield G., Peay J. and Player E. (1984) *Sentencing in the Crown Court: Report of an Exploratory Study.* Oxford, Centre for Criminological Research Occasional Paper No.10.

Aspden P. (1971) Unpublished Ph.D. thesis, Department of Operational Research, Lancaster University.

Aspen M.E. (1983) Judicial Function. In Kadish S.H. (ed) *Encyclopaedia of Crime and Justice*, vol.3. London, Collier-Macmillan.

Atiyah P.S. (1983) *Law and Modern Society.* Oxford, Oxford University Press.

Baird J. C. and Noma E. (1975) Psychological Study of Numbers: 1. Generation of Numerical Responses. *Psychological Research*, 37, 281–97.

Baldock J. C. (1980) Why the Prison Population has Grown Larger and Younger. *Howard Journal*, 19, 142–55.

Baldwin J. and McConville M. (1978) The Influence of the Sentencing Discount in Inducing Guilty Pleas. In Baldwin J. and Bottomley A. K., *Criminal Justice: Selected Readings*. Oxford, Martin Robertson.

Baldwin J. and McConville M. (1980) *Jury Trials*. Oxford, Martin Robertson.

Baxter R. and Nuttall C. P. (1975) Severe Sentences: No Deterrent to Crime? *New Society*, 31, 11–13.

Bem D. J. (1967) Self-Perception: An Alternative Interpretation of Cognitive Dissonance Phenomena. *Psychological Review*, 74, 183–200.

Bem D. J. and McConnell H. K. (1970) Testing the Self-Perception Explanation of Dissonance Phenomena: On the Salience of Pre-Manipulation Attitude. *Journal of Personality and Social Psychology*, 14, 23–31.

Beyleveld D. (1978) *The Effectiveness of General Deterrence Against Crime: An Annotated Bibliography of Evaluative Research*. University of Cambridge, Institute of Criminology.

Blackman D. (1981) On Mental Elements and their Place in Psychology and Law. In Shapland J. (ed.), Lawyers and Psychologists – The Way Forward. *Issues in Criminological and Legal Psychology*, 1. Leicester, British Psychological Society.

Bottomley A. K. (1980) The Justice Model in America and Britain: Development and Analysis. In Bottoms A. E. and Preston R. H., *The Coming Penal Crisis*. Edinburgh, Scottish Academic Press.

Bottoms A. E. (1981) The Suspended Sentence in England. *British Journal of Criminology*, 21, 1–26.

Bourdieu P. (1977) L'Économie des échanges linguistiques. *Lange Française*, 34, 17–34.

Bridge, Lord (1978) *Report of the Working Party on Judicial Studies and Information*. London, HMSO.

Brody S. (1976) *The Effectiveness of Sentencing*. Home Office Research Study No. 35, London, HMSO.

Brown R. W. (1956) Language and Categories. In Bruner J., Goodnow J. and Austin G., *A Study of Thinking*. New York, Science Editions.

Bryant J. W., Chambers M. L. and Falcon D. (1968) *Patrol Effectiveness and Patrol Deployment*. Department of Operational Research, Lancaster University.

Buchner D. (1979) Scale of Sentence Severity. *Journal of Criminal Law and Criminology*, 70, 182–7.

California Youth Authority (1975) *California's Probation Subsidy Programme*. Report No. 2, Sacramento, California.

California Youth Authority (1977) *An Evaluation of Seven Selected Probation Subsidy Programmes*. Sacramento, California.

Campbell D.T. and Stanley J.C. (1966) *Experimental and Quasi-Experimental Designs for Research*. Chicago, Rand McNally.

Carroll R.M., Pue S.M., Cline C.J. and Kleinhans B.R. (1974) Judged Seriousness of Watergate-Related Crimes. *Journal of Psychology*, 86, 235–9.

Chambers M.L. (1967) *Survey of Police Operations and Evaluations of their Effectiveness*. Department of Operational Research, Lancaster University.

Chambliss W.J. and Seidman R.B. (1971) *Law, Order and Power*. Reading, Addison-Wesley.

Champagne A. and Nagel S.S. (1982) The Psychology of Judging. In Kerr N.L. and Bray R.M. (eds), *The Psychology of the Courtroom*. New York, Academic Press.

Chapman L.J. and Chapman J.P. (1971) Test Results Are What You Think They Are. *Psychology Today*, November, 18–22, 106–10.

Chiricos T.G. and Waldo G.P. (1975) Socioeconomic Status and Criminal Sentencing: An Empirical Assessment of a Conflict Proposition. *American Sociological Review*, 40, 753–73.

Christiansen K.O., Kutschinsky M.B. and Karpatschof B. (1970) Method of Using an Index of Crime of the Kind Used by Sellin and Wolfgang. In *The Index of Crime: Some Further Studies*. European Committee on Crime Problems. Strasbourg, Council of Europe.

Clark W.W. (1922) *Whittier Scale for Grading Juvenile Offences*. California Bureau of Juvenile Research, Bulletin 11.

Cohen J. (1977) *The Probable and the Provable*. Oxford, Clarendon Press.

Cohen J. (1978) The Incapacitative Effect of Imprisonment: A Critical Review of the Literature. In Blumstein A., Cohen J. and Nagin D. (eds), *Deterrence and Incapacitation: Estimating the Effects of Criminal Sanctions on Crime Rates*. Washington, National Academy of Sciences.

Cook B. (1973) Sentencing Behaviour of Federal Judges – 1972. *University of Cincinnati Law Review*, 42, 567–633.

Coombs C.H. (1967) Thurstone's Measurement of Social Values Revised Forty Years Later. *Journal of Personality and Social Psychology*, 6, 85–91.

Crombag H.F.M., De Wijkerslooth J.L. and van Tuyl van Serooskerken E.H. (1975) On Solving Legal Problems. *Journal of Legal Education*, 27, 168–202.

Cross R. (1975) *The English Sentencing System*. London, Butterworth.

Cross R. (1981) *The English Sentencing System* (3rd edn). London, Butterworth.

Crow I. (1978) *Strategies for Reducing the Prison Population in Other Countries*. NACRO Information Sheet, August.

Crow I. (1980) Unemployment and Crime. Paper presented to a meeting of the Northern Ireland Association for the Care and Resettlement of Offenders, University Street, Belfast.

Crow I. and Cove J. (1984) Ethnic Minorities and the Courts. *Criminal Law Review*, July, 413–17.

Devlin P. (1965) *The Enforcement of Morals*. Oxford, Oxford University Press.

Devlin P. (1979) *The Judge*. Oxford, Oxford University Press.

Diamond S. S. and Herhold C. J. (1981) Understanding Criminal Sentencing: Views from Law and Social Psychology. In Stephenson G. M. and Davis J. M. (eds), *Progress in Applied Social Psychology*, vol. 1, Chichester, Wiley.

Duguid G. (1982) *Community Service in Scotland: The First Two Years*. Central Research Unit, Scottish Office, Edinburgh.

Durant M., Thomas M. and Willcock H. O. (1972) *Crime, Criminals and the Law*. London, OPCS.

Durea M. (1933) An Experimental Study of Attitudes Towards Juvenile Delinquency. *Journal of Applied Psychology*, 17, 522–34.

Durndell A. (1977) Does Psychology Support the Status Quo? *Bull. Brit. Psychol. Soc.*, 30, 320–2.

Eddy D. M. (1982) Probabilistic Reasoning in Clinical Medicine: Problems and Opportunities. In Kahneman D., Slovic P. and Tversky A. (eds), *Judgement under Uncertainty: Heuristics and Biases*. Cambridge, Cambridge University Press.

Einhorn H. J. (1980) Learning from Experience and Suboptimal Rules in Decision-Making. In Wallsten T. S. (ed.), *Cognitive Processes in Choice and Decision Behaviour*. Hillsdale NJ, Lawrence Erlbaum Associates.

Ericsson K. A. and Simon H. A. (1980) Verbal Reports as Data. *Psychological Review*, 87, 215–51.

Fairhead S. (1981) *Persistent Petty Offenders*. Home Office Research Study No. 66, London, HMSO.

Fallon P. (1975) *Crown Court Practice: Sentence*. London, Butterworth.

Farrington D. P. (1978) The Effectiveness of Sentences. *Justice of the Peace*, 4 February, 68–71.

Farrington D. P. and Hawkins K. (1978) Psychological Research on Behaviour in Legal Contexts. In Lloyd-Bostock S., Farrington D. P. and Hawkins K., *Psychology, Law and Legal Process*. London, Macmillan.

Farrington D. P. and Morris A. M. (1983) Sex, Sentencing and Reconviction. *British Journal of Criminology*, 23, 229–48.

Fischhoff B. (1975) Hindsight ≠ Foresight: The Effect of Outcome Knowledge on Judgment under Uncertainty. *Journal of Experimental Psychology: Human Perception and Performance*, 1, 288–99.

Fischhoff B. (1977) Perceived Informativeness of Facts. *Journal of Experimental Psychology: Human Perception and Performance*, 3, 349–58.

Fischhoff B. (1980) For Those Condemned to Study the Past: Reflections on Historical Judgment. In Schweder R. A. and Fiske D. W. (eds), *New Direction for the Methodology of Behavioural Science: Fallible Judgment in Behavioural Research*. San Francisco, Jossey-Bass.

Fischhoff B. and Beyth R. (1975) I Knew It Would Happen. Remembered Probabilities of Once-Future Things. *Organisational Behaviour and Human Performance*, 13, 1–16.

Fischhoff B., Lichtenstein S., Slovic P., Derby S. and Keeney R. (1981) *Acceptable Risk*. Cambridge, Cambridge University Press.

Fitzgerald M. and Sim J. (1979) *British Prisons*. Oxford, Blackwell.

Fitzmaurice C. (1981) On Measuring Distaste in Years: A Psychophysical Study of the Length of Prison Sentences. M.A. Econ. thesis, University of Manchester.

Flanagan J.C. (1954) The Critical Incident Technique. *Psychological Bulletin*, 51, 327–58.

Flegg D. (1976) *Consumer Survey 1973–6*, Nottingham, Nottinghamshire Probation and After-Care Service.

Forst M.L. (1982) Sentencing Disparity: An Overview of Research and Issues. In Forst M.L. (ed.), *Sentencing Reform: Experiments in Reducing Disparity*. Beverly Hills, Sage.

Frasure-Smith N., Lambert W. and Taylor D. (1975) Choosing the Language of Instruction of One's Children. *J. Cross-cultural Psychol.*, 6, 131–54.

Freud S. (1922) *Introductory Lectures on Psychoanalysis*. London, Allen & Unwin.

Galligan D.J. (1981) Guidelines and Just Deserts: A Critique of Recent Trends in Sentencing Reform. *Criminal Law Review*, 297–311.

Galton F. (1895) Terms of Imprisonment. *Nature*, 52, 174–6.

Ghiselin B. (1952) *The Creative Process*. New York, Mentor.

Gottfredson D.M. (1975) Diagnosis, Classification and Prediction. In Gottfredson D.M. (ed.), *Decision-Making in the Criminal Justice System: Reviews and Essays*. Rockville, National Institute of Mental Health.

Gottfredson D.M., Wilkins L.T. and Hoffman P.B. (1978) *Guidelines for Parole and Sentencing: A Policy Control Method*. Lexington, Heath.

Gottfredson M.R. and Gottfredson D.M. (1980) *Decision-Making in Criminal Justice: Towards the Rational Exercise of Discretion*. Cambridge, Mass., Ballinger.

Gottfredson S., Young, K.L. and Laufer W.S. (1980) Additivity and Interactions in Offence Seriousness Scales. *Journal of Research in Crime and Delinquency*, 17, 26–41.

Gray D.B. and Ashmore R.D. (1976) Biasing Influence of Defendants Characteristics on Simulated Sentencing. *Psychological Reports*, 38, 727–38.

Griffith J.A.G. (1977) *The Politics of the Judiciary*. London, Fontana.

Gross H. (1979) *A Theory of Criminal Justice*. New York, Oxford University Press.

Hagan J. (1974) Extra-legal Attributes and Criminal Sentencing: An Assessment of a Sociological Viewpoint. *Law and Society Review*, 8, 357–83.

Harland A.T. (1981) Court-ordered Community Service in Criminal Law: The Continuing Tyranny of Benevolence. *Buffalo Law Review*, 29, 425–86.

Hart H. L. A. (1968) *Punishment and Responsibility: Essays in the Philosophy of Law*. Oxford, Clarendon Press.

Herzberg F. I., Mausner B. and Snyderman B. B. (1957) *The Motivation to Work*. New York, Wiley.

Hjelle L. A. and Ziegler D. J. (1981) *Personality Theories: Basic Assumptions, Research and Application*. 2nd edn. New York, McGraw-Hill.

Hoffman P. B. (1972) Paroling Policy Feedback. *Journal of Research in Crime and Delinquency*, 9, 117–33.

Hoffman P. B. and Adelberg S. (1980) The Salient Factor Score: A Non-technical Overview. *Federal Probation*, March, 44–52.

Hogarth J. (1971) *Sentencing as a Human Process*. Toronto, University of Toronto Press.

Home Office (1977) *Review of Criminal Justice Policy 1976*. London, Home Office.

Hood R. (1962) *Sentencing in Magistrates Courts*. London, Stevens.

Hood R. (1972) *Sentencing the Motoring Offender*. London, Heinemann.

Hood R. (1974) *Tolerance and the Tariff*. London, NACRO.

House of Commons Expenditure Committee (1980) *15th Report*. London, HMSO.

Jackson R. M. (1971) *Enforcing the Law*. Harmondsworth, Penguin.

Jankovic I. (1978) Social Class and Criminal Sentencing. *Crime and Social Justice*, 10, 9–16.

Jardine E., Moore G. and Pease K. (1983) Community Service Orders, Employment and the Tariff. *Criminal Law Review*, 17–20.

Jenkins H. M. and Ward W. C. (1965) Judgments of Contingency between Responses and Outcomes. *Psychological Monographs*, 79.

Jones E. E. and Harris V. A. (1967) The Attribution of Attitudes. *Journal of Experimental Social Psychology*, 3, 1–24.

Kahneman D. and Tversky A. (1973) On the Psychology of Prediction. *Psychological Review*, 80, 237–51.

Kahneman D., Slovic P. and Tversky A. (eds) (1982) *Judgement under Uncertainty: Heuristics and Biases*. Cambridge, Cambridge University Press.

Kapardis A. and Farrington D. P. (1981) An Experimental Study of Sentencing by Magistrates. *Law and Human Behaviour*, 5, 107–21.

King M. (1984) Understanding the Legal System: A Job for Psychologists? In Müller D., Blackman D. and Chapman A. (eds), *Psychology and Law. Topics from an International Conference*. Chichester, Wiley.

King-Hamilton A. (1982) *And Nothing But the Truth*. London, Weidenfeld & Nicolson.

Kittrie N. N. (1971) *The Right to be Different: Deviance and Enforced Therapy*. Baltimore, Johns Hopkins University Press.

Knightley P. (1982) Judges Block Whitelaw on Sentencing in Courts. *Sunday Times*, 24 January.

Kress J. M. (1980) *Prescription for Justice: The Theory and Practice of Sentencing Guidelines.* Cambridge, Mass., Ballinger.

Kress J., Wilkins L. T. and Gottfredson D. M. (1976) Is the End of Judicial Sentencing in Sight? *Judicature*, 60, 216–22.

Krus P. H. and Sherman P. L. (1977) Changing Values over Last Half-Century. Story of Thurstone's Crime Scales. *Psychological Reports*, 40, 207–11.

Lasswell H. (1948) *Power and Personality.* New York, Norton.

Lemert E. M. (1970) *Social Action and Legal Change: Revolution within the Juvenile Court.* Chicago, Aldine.

Lemon N. (1974) Training, Personality and Attitude as Determinants of Magistrates' Sentencing. *British Journal of Criminology*, 14, 34–48.

Lemon N. (1975) Linguistic Development and Conceptualisation: A Bilingual Study. *J. Cross-Cultural Psychol.*, 6, 173–89.

Lerman P. (1975) *Community Treatment and Social Control.* Chicago, University of Chicago Press.

Lerner M. J. (1970) The Desire for Justice and Reactions to Victims – In Macauley J. and Berkowitz L. (eds), Altruism and Helping Behaviour. New York, Academic Press.

Lerner M. J. and Matthews G. (1967) Reactions to Suffering of Others under Conditions of Indirect Responsibility. *Journal of Personality and Social Psychology*, 5, 319–25.

Lesieur H. R. and Lehman P. M. (1975) Remeasuring Delinquency: A Replication and Critique. *British Journal of Criminology*, 15, 69–80.

Leventhal G. and Krate R. (1977) Physical Attractiveness and Severity of Sentencing. *Psychological Reports*, 40, 315–18.

Lewis T. J. and Habert B. (1983) Larvatus Prodeo. In Durard J. (ed.), *A Festschrift for Peter Wexler.* University of Essex Department of Language and Linguistics. Occasional Papers No. 27, 195–220.

Lichtenstein S., Fischhoff B. and Phillips L. D. (1977) Calibration of Probabilities: The State of the Art. In Jungerman H. and de Zeeuw G. (eds), *Decision-Making and Change in Human Affairs.* Amsterdam, Reidel.

Lipton D., Martinson R. and Wilks J. (1974) *The Effectiveness of Correctional Treatment.* New York, Praeger.

Lizotte A. J. (1978) Extra-legal Factors in Chicago's Criminal Courts: Testing the Conflict Model of Criminal Justice. *Social Problems*, 25, 564–80.

Lovegrove A. (in press) Judges, Sentencing and Experimental Psychology. *Journal of Community Psychology.*

Mackay J. G. and Rook M. K. (1976) *An Evaluation of Tasmania's Work Order Scheme.* Tasmania Probation and Parole Department.

Marshall J. (1974) *How to Survive in the Nick.* London, Allison & Busby.

Mayr G. (1867) Statistik der gerichtlichen Polizei im Königreiche Bayern und in einigen anderen Ländern, Munich, K. Statist. Bureau.

McConville M. and Baldwin J. (1982) The Influence of Race on Sentencing in England. *Criminal Law Review*, 652–8.

McFatter R. M. (1978) Sentencing Strategies and Justice: Effects of Punishment Philosophy on Sentencing Decisions. *Journal of Personality and Social Psychology*, 36, 1490–1500.

McKnight C. (1981) Subjectivity in Sentencing. *Law and Human Behaviour*, 5, 141–7.

McLean I. (1980) *Crown Court: Patterns of Sentencing*. Chichester, Barry Rose.

McWilliams W. W. (1975) Some Male Offenders' Problems: 1. Homeless Offenders in Liverpool. *Home Office Research Study No. 28*, London, HMSO.

Messedaglia A. (1866) Esposizione critica delle statistiche criminali dell'Impero austriaco. *Atti dell'I.R. Instituto Veneto di Scienze. Letteri ed Arti* 11, 153–211, 311–409, 483–510, 601–52, 993–1051, 1237–58.

Minnesota Department of Corrections (1979) *The Community Corrections Act*. St Paul, Minnesota.

Minnesota Department of Corrections (1980) *Dodge, Fillmore and Olmstead Counties Community Corrections System. Comprehensive Plan*. Olmstead County Courthouse, Rochester, Minnesota.

Mugford S. and Gronfors M. (1978) Racial and Class Factors in Sentencing of First Offenders. *Australian and New Zealand Journal of Criminology*, 14, 58–61.

Nagel S. S. (1962) Political Party Affiliation and Judges' Decisions. *American Political Science Review*, 55, 843–50.

Neugarten B. L. (1977) Adult Personality: Toward a Psychology of the Life-Cycle. In Allman L. R. and Jaffe D. T. (eds), *Readings in Adult Psychology: Contemporary Perspectives*. New York, Harper & Row.

Nisbett R. E. and Ross L. (1980) *Human Inference: Strategies and Short-comings of Social Judgement*. Englewood Cliffs NJ, Prentice-Hall.

Nisbett R. E. and Schachter S. (1966) Cognitive Manipulation of Pain. *Journal of Experimental Social Psychology*, 2, 227–36.

Nisbett R. E. and Wilson T. D. (1977) Telling More Than We Can Know: Verbal Reports on Mental Processes. *Psychological Review*, 84, 231–59.

Normandeau A. (1970) A Comparative Study of the Weighted Crime Indices for Eight Countries. *Revue Internationale de Police Criminelle*, 25, 15–18.

Northern Ireland Office (1984) *A Commentary on Northern Ireland Crime Statistics 1969–82*. PPRU Occasional Paper No. 5.

Nuttall C. P. with Barnard E. E., Fowles A. J., Frost A., Hammond W. H., Mayhew P., Pease K., Tarling R. and Weatheritt M. J. (1977) Parole in England and Wales. *Home Office Research Study No. 38*, London, HMSO.

Oatham E. and Simon F. (1972) Are Suspended Sentences Working? *New Society*, 3 August, 233–5.

Oddie C. (1984) Law and Psychology: A Personal View. In Müller D. J., Blackman D. E. and Chapman A. J. (eds), *Psychology and Law*. Chichester, Wiley.

Oskamp S. (1965) The Relationship of Clinical Experience and Training Methods to Several Criteria of Clinical Prediction. *Psychological Monographs*, 76.

Parker, M. A. (1980) *Community Service Orders: Interviews with Offenders in Inverclyde and Dunbarton 1978–9*. Statistics and Information Office, Social Work Department, Argyll–Dunbarton Division.

Parliamentary All-Party Penal Affairs Group (1980) *Too Many Prisoners*. London, Barry Rose.

Parliamentary All-Party Penal Affairs Group (1981). Still Too Many Prisoners. Mimeo, NACRO, London.

Pattenden R. (1984) The Power of the Criminal Division of the Court of Appeal to Depart from its own Precedents. *Criminal Law Review*, October, 592–603.

Pease K. (1979) *Reflections on the Development of Crime Prevention Strategies and Techniques in Western Europe, Excluding Roman Law Countries*. Report to CSDHA, United Nations, New York.

Pease K. (1980) *Prison Population*. Milton Keynes, Open University Press.

Pease K. (1981) The Size of the Prison Population. *British Journal of Criminology*, 21, 70–4.

Pease K. and Sampson M. (1977) Doing Time and Marking Time. *Howard Journal*, 16, 59–64.

Pease K. and Wolfson J. (1979) Incapacitation Studies: A Review and Commentary. *Howard Journal*, 18, 160–7.

Pease K., Billingham S. and Thorpe J. (1977) Community Service Assessed in 1976. *Home Office Research Study No. 39*, London, HMSO.

Pease K., Ireson J. and Thorpe J. (1974) Additivity Assumptions in the Measurement of Delinquency. *British Journal of Criminology*, 14, 256–63.

Pease K., Durkin P., Earnshaw I., Payne D. and Thorpe J. (1975) Community Service Orders. *Home Office Research Study, No. 29*, London, HMSO.

Pease K., Ireson J. and Thorpe J. (1975) Modified Crime Indices for Eight Countries. *Journal of Criminal Law, Criminology and Police Science*, 66, 209–21.

Pease K., Ireson J., Billingham S. and Thorpe J. (1976) The Development of a Scale of Offence Seriousness. *International Journal of Criminology and Penology*, 4, 1–13.

Petersilia S. (1980) Criminal Career Research: A Review of Recent Evidence. In Morris N. and Tonry M. (eds), *Crime and Justice: An Annual Review of Research*, 2, 321–79.

Philpotts, G. J. O. and Lancucki B. (1979) Previous Convictions, Sentence and Reconviction: A Statistical Study of a Sample of 500 Offenders

Convicted in January 1971. *Home Office Research Study No. 53*, London, HMSO.

Polonoski M. (1980) *The Community Service Order Programme in Ontario: Participants and their Perceptions*. Planning and Research Branch, Ontario Ministry of Correctional Services.

Polonoski M. (1981) *The Community Service Order Programme in Ontario: Summary*. Planning and Research Branch, Ontario Ministry of Correctional Services.

Pugsley R. A. (1979) Retributivism − A Just Basis for Criminal Sentences. *Hofstra Law Review*, 7, 379–405.

Rawls J. (1971) *A Theory of Justice*. Oxford, Oxford University Press.

Reidel M. (1975) Perceived Circumstances, Inferences of Intent and Judgments of Offence Seriousness. *Journal of Criminal Law, Criminology and Police Science*, 66, 201–8.

Rook M. K. (1978a) A Practical Evaluation of the Tasmanian Work Order Scheme. M.A. thesis, University of Tasmania.

Rook M. K. (1978b) Tasmania's Work Order Scheme: A Reply to Varne. *Australia and New Zealand Journal of Criminology*, 11, 81–8.

Rose G. N. G. (1966) Concerning the Measurement of Delinquency. *British Journal of Criminology*, 6, 414–21.

Ross L., Amabile T. M. and Steinmetz J. L. (1977) Social Roles, Social Control and Biases in Social Perception Processes. *Journal of Personality and Social Psychology*, 35, 485–94.

Ross L., Greene D. and House P. (1977) The False Consensus Phenomenon: An Attributional Bias in Self Perception and Social Perception Processes. *Journal of Experimental Social Psychology*, 13, 279–301.

Rossi P. H., Waite E., Bose C. E. and Berk R. E. (1974) The Seriousness of Crimes: Normative Sturcture and Individual Differences. *American Sociological Review*, 39, 224–37.

Rubin S. (1966) Disparity and Equality of Sentence: A Constitutional Challenge. *Federal Rules Decisions*, 55, 65–7.

Russell B. (1950) *Unpopular Essays*. London, Allen & Unwin.

Saks M. J. and Hastie L. (1978) *Social Psychology in Court*. New York, Van Nostrand.

Schum D. A. (1980) Current Developments in Research on Cascaded Inference Processes. In Wallsten T. S. (ed.), *Cognitive Processes in Choice and Decision Behaviour*. Hillsdale NJ, Lawrence Erlbaum Associates.

Sebba L. (1969) Penal Reform and Court Practice: The Case of the Suepended Sentence. *Scripta Hierosolymitana*, 21, 133–48.

Sebba L. (1978) Some Explorations in the Scaling of Penalties. *Journal of Research in Crime and Delinquency*, 15, 247–65.

Sebba L. and Nathan G. (1984) Further Explorations in the Scaling of Penalties. *British Journal of Criminology*, 23, 221–49.

Sellin, T. and Wolfgang M. (1964) *The Measurement of Delinquency*. New York, Wiley.

Shapland J. M. (1981) *Between Conviction and Sentence*. London, Routledge & Kegan Paul.

Shaver R. (1975) *An Introduction to Attribution Processes*, New York, Winthrop.

Shaw S. (1983) *Community Service: A Guide for Sentencers*. London, Prison Reform Trust.

Sherman R. C. and Dowdle M. D. (1974) The Perception of Crime and Punishment: A Multidimensional Scaling Analysis. *Social Science Research*, 3, 109–26.

Shitrit S. (1972) The Impact of the Personality of the Judge in Sentencing Policy. *Criminology, Criminal Law and Police Science*, 1, 125–45.

Skinner B. F. (1971) *Beyond Freedom and Dignity*. Harmondsworth, Pelican.

Smedslund J. (1963) The Concept of Correlation in Adults. *Scandinavian Journal of Psychology*, 4, 165–73.

Smedslund J. (1966) Note on Learning, Contingency and Clinical Experience. *Scandinavian Journal of Psychology*, 7, 265–6.

Sophocles (trans. 1940) *The Theban Plays*. Harmondsworth, Pelican.

Sparks R. F. (1971) The Use of Suspended Sentences. *Criminal Law Review*, 384–401.

Sparks R. F. (1983) Sentencing Guidelines. In Kadish S. H., *Encyclopaedia of Crime and Justice*. London, Collier-Macmillan.

Sparks R. F., Genn H. and Dodd D. (1977) *Surveying Victims*. Chichester, Wiley.

Stecher B. A. and Sparks R. F. (1982) Removing the Effects of Discrimination in Sentencing Guidelines. In Forst M. L. (ed.), *Sentencing Reform: Experiments in Reducing Disparity*. Beverly Hills, Sage.

Stevens S. S. (1971) Issues in Psychophysical Measurement. *Psychological Review*, 78, 426–50.

Stevens S. S. (1975) *Psychophysics: Introduction to its Perceptual, Neural and Social Aspects*. Chichester, Wiley.

Stewart J. E. (1980) Defendant's Attractiveness as a Factor in the Outcome of Criminal Trials: An Observational Study. *Journal of Applied Social Psychology*, 10, 348–61.

Storms M. D. and Nisbett R. E. (1970) Insomnia and the Attribution Process. *Journal of Personality and Social Psychology*, 16, 319–28.

Streatfeild Report (1961) *Report of the Interdepartmental Committee on the Business of the Criminal Courts*. London, HMSO.

Tarling R. (1980) Sentencing Practice in Magistrates Courts. *Home Office Research Study No. 56*, London, HMSO.

Taylor L. (1972) The Significance and Interpretation of Replies to Motivational Questions: The Case of Sex Offenders. *Sociology*, 6, 23–39.

Thomas D. A. (1963) Sentencing – The Case for Reasoned Decisions. *Criminal Law Review*, 243–54.

Thomas D. A. (1978a) *Constraints on Judgement*. Cambridge, Institute of Criminology.

Thomas D. A. (1978b) *The Penal Equation*. Institute of Criminology, Cambridge.

Thomas D. A. (1979a) *Principles of Sentencing* (2nd edn). London, Heinemann.

Thomas D. A. (1979b) *The Future of Sentencing*. Institute of Criminology, Cambridge.

Thomas D. A. (1983) Sentencing Discretion and Appellate Review. In Shapland J. (ed.), *Decision Making in the Legal System. Issues in Criminological and Legal Psychology*, 5, 61–71.

Thorpe J. (1978) Social Inquiry Reports. *Home Office Reseach Study No. 48*, London, HMSO.

Thurstone L. L. (1927) The Method of Paired Comparisons for Social Values. *Journal of Abnormal and Social Psychology*, 21, 384–400.

Tversky A. and Kahneman D. (1973) Availability: a Heuristic for Judging Frequency and Probability. *Cognitive Psychology*, 4, 207–32.

Tversky A. and Kahneman D. (1974) Judgement under Uncertainty: Heuristics and Biases. *Science*, 185, 1124–31.

Tversky A. and Kahneman D. (1982) Causal Schemas in Judgements under Uncertainty. In Kahneman D., Slovic P. and Tversky A. (eds), *Judgement under Uncertainty: Heuristics and Biases*. Cambridge, Cambridge University Press.

van Dijk J. (1983) The Use of Guidelines by Prosecutors in the Netherlands. In Shapland J. (ed.), *Decision Making in the Legal System: Issues in Criminological and Legal Psychology*, 5, 38–49.

Van Dine S., Dinitz S. and Conrad J. (1977) The Incapacitation of the Dangerous Offender: A Statistical Experiment. *Journal of Research in Crime and Delinquency*, 14, 22–34.

Vass A. A. (1984) *Sentenced to Labour*. St Ives, Venus Academica.

Velez-Diaz A. and Megargee E. I. (1970) An Investigation of Differences in Value Judgements between Youthful Offenders and Non-Offenders in Puerto Rico. *Journal of Criminal Law, Criminology and Police Science*, 61, 549–53.

Von Hirsch A. (1976) *Doing Justice: The Choice of Punishment*. New York, Hill & Wang.

Wagner H. L. and Pease K. (1978) On Adding Up Scores of Offence Seriousness. *British Journal of Criminology*, 18, 175–8.

Walker M. (1978) Measuring the Seriousnes of Crimes. *British Journal of Criminology*, 18, 348–64.

Walker N. (1971) Psychophysics and the Recording Angel. *British Journal of Criminology*, 11, 191–4.

Walker N. (1980) *Punishment, Danger and Stigma*. Oxford, Blackwell.

Walker N. (1981) A Note on Parole and Sentence Lengths. *Criminal Law Review*, 829–30.

Walker N. and Marsh C. (1984) Do Sentences Affect Public Disapproval? *British Journal of Criminology*, 24, 27–48.

Wallsten T.S. (ed.) (1980) *Cognitive Processes in Choice and Decision Behavior*. Hillsdale NJ, Lawrence Erlbaum Associates.

Ward W.C. and Jenkins H.M. (1965) The Display of Information and the Judgement of Contingency. *Canadian Journal of Psychology*, 19, 231–41.

Wardlaw G. (1978) Drug Use and Crime: An Examination of Drug Users and Associated Persons and their Influence on Crime Patterns in Australia. Mimeo, Australian Institute of Criminology, Woden ACT, Australia 2606.

Wasik M. (1982) Reflections on Sentencing Guidelines. *Justice of the Peace*, 146, 771–3.

Wason P.C. (1960) On the Failure to Eliminate Hypotheses: A Conceptual Task. *Quarterly Journal of Experimental Psychology*, 23, 63–71.

Weber E.H. (1846) Der Tastsinn und das Gemeinfühl. In Wagner R., *Handwörterbuch der Physiologie*, vol. 3. Vieweg, Braunschweig.

Wellford C.F. and Wiatrowski M. (1975) On the Measurement of Delinquency. *Journal of Criminal Law and Criminology*, 66, 175–88.

Wheeler S., Bonacich E., Cromer M.R. and Zola I.K. (1968) Agents of Delinquency Control: A Comparative Analysis. In Wheeler S. (ed.), *Controlling Delinquents*. New York, Wiley.

Whittington N. (1977) *Community Service by Offenders Survey*. Newcastle, Newcastle Polytechnic.

Wilkins L.T. (1980) *The Principles of Guidelines for Sentencing*. US Department of Justice, Washington.

Wilkins L.T. (1983) *Consumerist Criminology*. London, Heinemann.

Wilkins L.T. (1984) UK/USA Contrasts in Criminology: A Personal View. *Howard Journal*, 23, 11–23.

Wilkins L.T., Gottfredson D.M., Robison J.O. and Sadowsky C.A. (1972) *Information Selection and Use in Parole Decision-Making*. NCCD Research Center, Davis, California.

Willis A. (1977) Community Service as an Alternative to Imprisonment: A Cautionary View. *Probation Journal*, 24, 120–5.

Wood G. (1978) The Knew-It-All-Along Effect. *Journal of Experimental Psychology: Human Perception and Performance*, 4, 345–53.

Young, J. (1971) The Role of the Police as Amplifiers of Deviancy. In Cohen S. (ed.), *Images of Deviance*. Harmondsworth, Pelican.

Young, J. (1979) *Community Service Orders*. London, Heinemann.

Index